I AM

A Study of the True and Living God

Edited by
Jeremy W. Barrier

and

Charles R. Webb

Copyright © 2023 Reissued

Manufactured in the United States of America

Cataloging-in-Publication Data

I AM: a study of the true and living God / edited by Jeremy W. Barrier and Charles R. Webb

p. cm.

Includes scripture index.

ISBN 978-1-956811-37-7 (pbk.) 978-1-956811-38-4 (ebook)

1. God (Christianity). 2. God (Christianity)—Attributes. I. Barrier, Jeremy W., editor II. Webb, Charles R., editor. III. Title.

231.1—dc20

Library of Congress Control Number: 2022924076

Cover design by Brad McKinnon and Brittany Vander Maas.

For more information:

Cypress Publications
3625 Helton Drive
PO Box HCU
Florence, AL 35630

www.hcu.edu

Dedicated to PR and Saroja Swamy and their dream to tell the good news to all of India.

Acknowledgments

There are many who should be remembered, so we fear we will forget some. For this reason, we apologize to anyone we might overlook as this book approaches publication. First and foremost, thanks should be extended to the late JC and his widow Betty Choate, who have instilled a love for God in so many people throughout the world.

Thanks also to Wayne and Janet Barrier for introducing us to PR and Saroja Swamy for the first time. This project is the idea of PR Swamy, who has been trying to publish a book on God for the people of India for over 35 years now. Even the chapter divisions were his ideas.

Thanks also to Cory Collins who suggested we pursue this project in the English language for an American audience (we originally intended this only for an Indian audience), and to Heritage Press for taking on the American project. Thanks to Lori Eastep for editing the Indian edition into an edition appropriate for an American audience. Also, thanks go to the Jacks Creek Church of Christ (Jacks Creek, TN) who initially took on this project to help the Christians of India.

In particular, thanks go to Joe and Ramay Noles, who have been a constant source of encouragement in completing this project. Also, thanks go to our families as they are also a constant support and strength in every way. In particular, thank you Ruth and Robin.

Jeremy W. Barrier
Charles R. Webb
December 2009

Contents

Revealing I AM

Jeremy W. Barrier

Many times I have stood looking out toward the west and marveled at the beauty that I saw in the creation. As the radiant and brilliant sun set before my eyes, glowing in colors of intense red, orange, and yellow and contrasted by sky the color of a ripe mango filled with yellow, purple, and red, I would think to myself, "A truly magnificent God must have made this." I cannot help but marvel at the infinite detail of a grasshopper or the elaborate design that I see in the flowers upon the brilliant trees of Bangalore, India, so wonderfully called the "flame of the forest." There must be some kind of Divine Creator who could make this magnificent world.

Where does the energy of creation come from? Who placed each intricate feather on the wings of the birds? Who set the rivers and brooks to flow down magnificent mountains? It must be a God who has done this!

We know design when we see it. Have you ever walked into a field that has been planted with corn and noticed that someone has come through and disturbed the plants? We reason that it must have been a child or some animal that has come through and damaged the field. On the other hand, I have come home to find that it has been cleaned up—with the food, clothing, and other items in the house arranged—and I say to myself, "Someone has been cleaning here." Isn't this true also of creation, when we see all of the magnificent sites around us? We see the sun, the moon, the stars, the mountains, and then we say, "*Someone* made this." It must be God.

Once we realize that it is truly God who has made everything around us, we can begin our search to find out more about this God. I have often asked, "Has God spoken to humans or revealed Himself to us in any other way than simply allowing us to see Him in His creation?" In short, the answer is yes. I have come to realize that God has revealed Himself to us on a more personal level than simply creating the universe. God has attempted to talk with humans and establish a relationship with humans. From the very beginning of time, God has spoken to people through his special messengers, the prophets. Many prophets attempted to tell humans in past generations that God would like to have a close relationship with us, but few people believed those prophets.

However, in later times, God revealed Himself to humanity in a more direct way. God revealed Himself through manifesting Himself on this earth as a human who went by the name of Jesus. This Divine-man, Jesus, lived on the earth almost 2,000 years ago. He was very poor. He lived as a humble, hard-working carpenter, and after He reached the age of 30 years, He began to explain to everyone that He was God. How do I know this? I know this because I have come to trust and respect the words of the Bible. I have come to realize that the Bible is the actual words of God, and it tells us many things about God.

Within various different religions and cultures, certain pieces of literature have been revered as Scriptures from the Divine. Their followers have sought to know the Divine and to find out what the gods desire for them in their lives. Within Hinduism, the Vedas, the Upanishads, *Ramayana*, and the *Bhagavad Gita* attempt to point people to the Divine. Within Islam, the *Qur'an* is claimed by Muslims to be the actual words of Allah as spoken and recorded through Mohammed, the Prophet. And within the ancient religion of Zoroastrianism, the *Avestas*, the ancient "scriptures" written in an ancient Indo-European Iranian language, have been consulted by their priests as they have aimed to please the Divine.

Yet from the East, Christianity has sprung forth, influencing billions of people over the centuries and still having a tremendous impact all over the world today. A very important source within Christianity has always been the sacred Scriptures that we call the Bible. It is in this book, the Bible, that God chose to reveal to us the grand story of Jesus, along with the history of God's relationship to humanity. It is in this book that God has revealed, very specifically, His words, thoughts, motives, and feelings to us, so that we will understand how we can respond to Him.

As one proceeds into this book, I would like to instill in the reader a sense of wonder and awe—as if we are entering into the throne room of God, shedding our preconceived notions of God and simply falling before His throne as our knees buckle from trembling before His face. Who is this magnificent God who has revealed Himself to humanity through creation, and then specifically through the Bible? It is my desire that the reader will be able to approach this book, and with a fresh mind look at God, as if for the first time, so that we might truly marvel at the glory and bow our hearts before Him.

A few years ago, while I was in New Delhi, India, I remember visiting several families in the Defense Colony. As my native Indian friend, Vinay David, and I, along with my wife, Robin, and our friend Todd began to visit with people in some of the poorer neighborhoods, several conversations stood out in my mind. I remember talking to one Hindu man in his fifties, married with 11 children and living in a 10' x 10' one-room flat. Many of his children were sitting around him, along with his thin dog sitting just outside the opening of the door. His deep blue eyes pierced mine with his sorrow as he explained to me that he hoped to be born as a dog in his next life. I was confused ... wouldn't he want a better life next time? I asked him, "Why? Why is a dog's life better?" He then explained to us that if he were a dog, he would not have to work so hard in the next life. He could lie around with someone to feed him, and no one would bother him.

As I reflect on this man's life, I wonder if this is really all of the hope that we have to anticipate in life. The only difference between the man and me was my more privileged birth. Did God really intend for either of us to have so little to hope for? I think not. As you read through this volume, I hope that you are able to gain some appreciation for the Christian God, His love, His compassion, His nature, His presence, His might, and His mercy upon us as humans who face many obstacles in life. It is my hope that upon the completion of this book, you will be curious enough to look at the Bible for yourself to judge whether these things are so. God be with you in your search for Him, and may it be soon that you realize and understand that God has been seeking you long before you began to seek Him.

Knowing I AM

Charles R. Webb

T hink for a moment of the person that you know the best. It may be a spouse, a very close friend, a parent, or some other person. How did you learn so much about this individual? Some of your knowledge came from observation. Some of it came from other people who know this person, maybe even before you knew them. Most of your knowledge probably came from spending time with that person and by that person telling you about themselves. You know a great deal about this individual, but I am sure that there are some things that you do not know. There are probably things that happened to the person that you have not yet learned. There are also some things that you cannot know. For example, if the person is a woman and you are a man, you can never know what it was like for her to give birth to a child.

Think for a moment about me, the author of this chapter. You have probably guessed by my name that I am a man. Because I am writing this material you could guess that I believe in the God of the Bible, but beyond these few things you know little else about me. Let me tell you a few things about myself I have been married for 45 years. My wife and I have three biological children (two boys and a girl) and one adopted daughter. I am a retired college professor, which implies that I have received advanced education. I could go on listing various characteristics of myself, but if you knew every characteristic about me you still would not really know me. You would not know what kind of husband, father or teacher I have been. You would not know my deepest desires and feelings, or what I value in life.

This chapter is entitled "Knowing God." First let me issue a caution. Knowing God is similar to knowing another person, but it is also very different. This can be stated differently as: God can be known but not comprehended. Because God is a person, He can be known as other persons are known. But God is a person which is far different than a human being. "God's voice thunders in marvelous ways; He does great things beyond our understanding" (Job 37:5). "Oh, the depth of the riches of the wisdom and knowledge of God! How unsearchable His judgments, and His paths beyond tracing out" (Romans 11:33)! "Beyond all question, the mystery of godliness is great" (1 Timothy 3:16). "Holy, holy, holy is the LORD Almighty; the whole earth is full of His glory" (Isaiah 6:3).

Although God is knowable, these and numerous other passages refer to the fact that as humans we can never comprehend God. Ephesians 3:18–19 is a good example of this tension. "That you may have power, together with all the saints, to grasp how wide and long and high and deep is the love of Christ, and to know this love that surpasses knowledge—that you may be filled to the measure of all the fullness of God." In this passage Paul says that we may know the love of Christ, yet he also says that the love of Christ surpasses knowledge; that is, the love of Christ is knowable but incomprehensible.

Now back to the person that you know the best. We know God the same way that we know another person. By observing nature we become aware of the existence of God. Through the scripture, God's revelation of Himself and His relationship with humans, we not only become aware of God but we also learn many of the characteristics of God which are discussed in the following chapters of this book. And in addition, from the Bible we learn many other things about God, including the majesty, glory, and incomparable nature of God and that He is above all other gods. "Declare His glory among the nations, His marvelous works among all the peoples! For great is the LORD, and greatly to be praised, and He is to be held in awe above all gods" (1 Chronicles 16:24–25).

But just as there are some things you may never know about another person, the same is true of God. This may be true for two reasons. First, God did not choose to reveal certain things about Himself. There are some things that humans cannot know or deal with regarding God; for example, seeing God face to face while we are in this human form (Exodus 33:18–23). Second, there are many things about God that are simply beyond our comprehension—partly because we are finite and God is infinitely great. For example, we cannot fully understand how God can be one God, yet exist in three personalities as the

Father, Son, and Holy Spirit. Or how Jesus, God living in human form upon the earth, could be both fully God and fully human at the same time. The deity of Jesus Christ is seen in the following passage: "The Son is the radiance of God's glory and the exact representation of His being, sustaining all things by His powerful word. After He had provided purification for sins, He sat down at the right hand of the Majesty in heaven" (Hebrews 1:3). The humanity of Jesus is explained in Hebrews 4:14–15:

Therefore, since we have a great high priest who has gone through the heavens, Jesus the Son of God, let us hold firmly to the faith we profess. For we do not have a high priest who is unable to sympathize with our weaknesses, but we have one who has been tempted in every way, just as we are—yet was without sin.

We can only exclaim with Paul and Job:

Oh, the depth of the riches of the wisdom and knowledge of God! How unsearchable his judgments, and his paths beyond tracing out! (Romans 11:33)

God's voice thunders in marvelous ways; he does great things beyond our understanding. (Job 37:5)

Now back to thinking about me, the author of this chapter. I listed several characteristics about myself, but a person is more than the sum of his or her characteristics. For instance, from what I said about myself above, the facts do not tell you whether I am a very patient or loving person. There are many significant things about a person that you would not know about them if you only have a list of his characteristics. This is true even if the list contains some very important characteristics, such as love. The same is true of God. As we continue to read the Bible and learn more and more about God, we learn that He is more than eternal, all powerful and the other important characteristics covered in this book In other words, we get beyond understanding God just in terms of a list of characteristics.

One of the things that we learn is that the most common description of God in the Bible is as a father. This immediately gives us insight into the nature of God. Even if you did not have a good earthly father or have unpleasant memories of your earthly father, you probably know what a good father is supposed to be. A father is one who loves his children, cares for his children, and only desires the very best for them in life. Think for a moment of the very best possible earthly father you can imagine. God is that and so much more. He is the perfect father in every way. Because He is a father, we can approach Him as one of His children, confident that when we need Him, He will help us to better handle the problems of life that we encounter.

God is also revealed as one who is faithful to the promises He has made and one who is trustworthy. But the most complete revelation of God is in Jesus Christ. This is where God and humans meet because Jesus was both God and a man. John refers to Jesus Christ as the Word—the revealer of God in the flesh. "For God was pleased to have all His fullness dwell in him (Colossians 1:19)," This is clearly seen in the following exchange between Jesus and Philip in John 14:6–11.

> Jesus answered, "I am the way and the truth and the life. No one comes to the Father except through me. If you really knew me, you would know my Father as well. From now on, you do know him and have seen him." Philip said, "Lord, show us the Father and that will be enough for us." Jesus answered: "Don't you know me, Philip, even after I have been among you such a long time? Anyone who has seen me has seen the Father. How can you say, 'Show us the Father?' Don't you believe that I am in the Father, and that the Father is in me? The words I say to you are not just my own. Rather, it is the Father, living in me, who is doing his work. Believe me when I say that I am in the Father and the Father is in me."

Knowing God is intimately related to knowing Jesus. Notice the critical nature of knowing God and Jesus in this prayer of Jesus to His Father: "Now this is eternal life: that they may know You, the only true God and Jesus Christ whom You have sent" (John 17:3). And again Jesus said, "All things have been committed to me by my Father. No one knows the Son except the Father, and no one knows the Father except the Son and those to whom the Son chooses to reveal Him" (Matthew 11:27). By carefully reading and meditating on the four gospels (Matthew, Mark, Luke, and John at the beginning of the New Testament) we can learn of the ways in which God relates to humans through the way Jesus related to people when He lived on the earth. For example, Jesus always had time for people because people are more important than things to God. He was never so busy doing other things that He did not stop and take time to interact with each person who approached Him. Jesus is the clearest revelation of God's love for each of us. The willingness of Jesus to die on the cross as the means of bringing man into a loving relationship with God opens a window for us into the very heart of God.

Another thing that we learn from Jesus and from reading the Bible in general is that God is a giving God. Yes, it is true that God asks or requires certain things of us, but it is also true that He is willing to help and bless us when we live in relationship with Him. "Give and it will be given to you. A good measure, pressed down, shaken together and running over, will be poured into your lap. For with the measure you use, it will be measured to you" (Luke 6:38). In the last paragraph we learned of God giving His Son for our sins, and in this passage of scripture we see that God gives in other ways as well.

One of the most attractive things about God is that He values each human being equally. Every human—male or female, rich or poor, educated or uneducated, upper class or lower class, well-dressed or poorly-dressed—is of equal value in God's sight. "I now realize how true it is that God does not show favoritism but accepts men from every nation who fear him and do what is right" (Acts 10:34–35). James, in his short book, encourages us to behave in the same way.

My brothers, as believers in our glorious Lord Jesus Christ, don't show favoritism. Suppose a man comes into your meeting wearing a gold ring and fine clothes, and a poor man in shabby clothes also comes in. If you show special attention to the man wearing fine clothes and say, "Here's a good seat for you," but say to the poor man, "You stand there" or "Sit on the floor by my feet," have you not discriminated among yourselves and become judges with evil thoughts? (James 2:1–4)

To understand the equality of all human beings, we must see other people the way God sees them. Every human being is created in the image of God. "God said, 'Let us make man in our image'... So God created man in his own image, in the image of God he created him; male and female he created them" (Genesis 1:26–27). Since every person is created in the image of God, just as I am, then each deserves the love from us that God commanded. In other words, every human being is of equal value in the sight of God. Whether one is the ruler of a nation or the poorest untouchable in the world, all are equally loved by God. To be created in the image of God is a wonder beyond our understanding. Yet each person is created in the image of God, which makes each person valuable beyond anything else on earth, and even beyond all the earth and everything in it. How can we measure the worth of anything created in the image of God, which is an everlasting soul?

In relation to knowing God, as in the examples of the equality of worth of all human beings, there are two extremes that we should avoid. The first is the idea that God is so great and incomprehensible that we cannot know Him ... that is, He is so transcendent, above and completely beyond us, that He is unknowable by humans.

The second extreme is the idea that we can know God completely because He is immanent, that is, because He is very close to us or near us. Humans can never fully know or master God through gaining knowledge of Him. Both extremes are equally damaging in our approach to knowing God and in both situations we greatly distort a true knowledge of God. As was said earlier, God can be known but never comprehended.

We can learn much about God by reading the Bible, but to truly understand and know God we must experience God just as we have experienced those on earth that we really know and love. Up to this point, we have been talking about knowing God by the various ways He is revealed to us. The ultimate way of knowing God is through experiencing God in our daily lives because we have or we want to establish a relationship with God. For example, I really enjoy fishing and I have several books about fishing. I could read and study all about fishing. I could learn all the principles of casting and how to manipulate my bait so that a fish will take it. But unless I actually go fishing and experience the thrill of having a fish come to the top of the water and taking my bait, I have missed the whole point of learning about fishing. The same is true of God. We can read and meditate on the scriptures and learn all that we can about God, but until we experience God through seeking a relationship with Him we will never really understand Him.

We experience God in many different ways. One of the ways is to experience God through His wonderful love

And I pray that you, being rooted and established in love, may have power, together with all the saints, to grasp how wide and long and high and deep is the love of Christ, and to know this love that surpasses knowledge —that you may be filled to the measure of all the fullness of God (Ephesians 3:17–19).

Notice that this is a love that surpasses knowledge. In other words, it is not based on just knowledge of God (of course we must have a knowledge of God to know Him) but implies a close relationship with God based on having experienced Him. The difference between knowledge of God and knowing God is that knowledge of God is more mental and rational, whereas knowing God is more attitudinal and experiential.

This difference is very important. Knowing about someone may lead to respect, but it will never lead to a meaningful relationship with the person. In fact, a separation between knowing about God and knowing God in our lives leads to a separation between knowledge. and relationships. God seeks to draw us into a loving relationship with Him. "'But I, when I am lifted up from the earth, will draw all men to myself.' He said this to show the kind of death he was going to die" (John 12:32–33). Here we see God's desire and the extent to which He is willing to go to draw each of us into a loving relationship with Him.

We can also experience God by being aware of how much He cares for us and the way He takes care of us. Some authors of the Old Testament help us understand how much God loves and cares for each of us. We have two beautiful portraits of God's care for us in Isaiah and the

Psalms. "He tends His flock like a shepherd: He gathers the lambs in His arms and carries them close to His heart; He gently leads those that have young" (Isaiah 40:11). "You hold me by my right hand" (Psalm 73:23). In these two beautiful and endearing passages, we see in an intimate way that God cares for us. It is as a shepherd's gentle way with the lambs and ewes in His care, and a father holding a child's hand. As we come to know God, we learn that there is no limit to the love of God or to the persistence of God's love for us. God's hand is always there for us. He is there just beyond the thin veil that separates this physical world from the spiritual. We can, figuratively, just reach through the veil and take hold of God's hand whenever we need or want to.

In this chapter, the discussion has been mostly about understanding God, the Father, and how He is revealed to us through God, the Son—Jesus Christ. God, the Holy Spirit is also involved in knowing God. The Father, Son, and Holy Spirit are the three personalities of the one God —three in one and one in three. This is part of the mystery of God. The Holy Spirit guided the writers of the Bible as they revealed God's actions and message to man. He is further involved in our knowing God because He (the Holy Spirit) helps to open the meaning and truth of the Bible to us as we read it. And when we enter into a relationship to God as one of His children, the Holy Spirit dwells within each Christian and helps us to understand God more fully as we experience God in our lives.

However, as it is written: 'No eye has seen, no ear has heard, no mind has conceived what God has prepared for those who love him'—but God has revealed it to us by his Spirit. The Spirit searches all things, even the deep things of God. For who among men knows the thoughts of a man except the man's spirit within him? In the same way no one knows the thoughts of God except the Spirit of God. We have not received the spirit of the world but the Spirit who is from God, that we may understand what God has freely given us. This is what we speak, not in words taught us by human wisdom but in words taught by the Spirit, expressing spiritual truths in spiritual words. The man without the Spirit does not accept the things that come from the Spirit of God, for they are foolishness to him, and he cannot understand them, because they are spiritually discerned (1 Corinthians 2:9–14).

Questions for Thought and Discussion

1. Is it possible for us to fully know God? Why or why not?
2. What are some things we do not/cannot know about God?
3. What characteristics of ourselves show us some characteristics of God?
4. What extremes should we avoid when seeking to know God? Why?
5. Which is more important—having a knowledge of God or knowing God? Can either exist without the other?

Who Created I AM?

Kevin J. Youngblood

Every human suffers from an insatiable curiosity regarding his or her origins. Normally this curiosity is expressed in a deep and abiding interest in our ancestry. We love to hear stories about our family, stories about ancestors who participated in great historical events, stories about the heroic deeds of our great-grandmothers and great-grandfathers. Why do humans share this universal curiosity about our family ancestry? I think it is because we gain a sense of identity from our ancestors. We realize that many people contribute to who we are. Many of our characteristics were "forced" on us. We did not choose them. This goes for more than just obvious things like eye color, hair color, and skin color. This applies even to personality traits such as intelligence, creativity, and our propensity for certain likes and dislikes.

This interest in our origins, however, extends beyond family heritage. It extends even to the ultimate questions of human origin. Where did we all come from? Where did the first human come from? Can all humans ultimately trace their ancestry back to one common ancestor? Such questions strike at the very heart of our identity and energize our quest for self-understanding.

Somehow we humans know that we are not selfexplanatory; we are not the beginning or the source of all things. But if we are not, then who or what is? Many worldviews would answer this question with a single word—God. This, however, raises the obvious question of where God came from. Who created God? Does he have parents? Can he trace his genealogy? Of course, different people will answer these questions in different ways. Some views of God simply lead to yet another endless cycle of origins in which one god conceives and gives birth to another god and so on, and so on indefinitely. The Biblical view of God, however, is different. The Bible affirms that God had no beginning. His existence is not dependent on anything or anyone outside of Himself. Psalm 90:2 states this clearly and succinctly: "Before the mountains were brought forth, or ever you had fonned the earth and the world, from everlasting to everlasting you are God."

Just as the dependence of our existence on a genealogy or family tree is basic to our identity, so the radical independence of God's existence and His lack of origin are basic to His identity. In fact, the very name by which God refers to Himself and by which He asks His people to refer to Him expresses the centrality of His independent existence to His self-understanding. God revealed to Moses in Exodus 3:14 that His name is "I AM." He is the great "I AM," timeless, without beginning or end, always fully present in the present because His name in the Hebrew language (the language of the Old Testament) is the present tense of the verb "to be."

It is difficult for humans, for whom origin is such an integral and important part of our identity, to conceive of a being who has no origin. We are tempted to wonder whether a being who has no origin can even have an identity. That is precisely what this book is about. This book serves as a kind of introduction to the God who reveals Himself in the Bible as the "the First and the Last," "the Alpha and the Omega," "the Beginning and the End" (Isaiah 48:12; Revelation 1:17; 22:13). All of these are self-designations God uses to assert the radical independence of His existence, the fact that He was not created, has no beginning, is without genealogy. We may not be self-explanatory, but God is. We may not be selfsustaining, but God is. We may need a beginning, a source, a reason for our existence, but the true God, as told about in the Bible, does not.

This realization raises a second important question. If we cannot know God on the basis of His origin, or His "family ancestry," then on what basis can we know Him? We are so accustomed to relating to people on the basis of their family background, or where they came from that we are unsure how to go about relating to and understanding a being, a person who has no ancestry, no parents, no heritage.

At this point, the Bible makes a crucial distinction. The fact that God has no beginning and no origin does not mean that He has no story. God does indeed have a story, and it is through this story that God reveals Himself to us.

It is on the basis of this story that we understand the nature of this God who had no beginning but is the beginning of all things, who did not come from a family but who creates families and places us within them (Psalm 68:6; Ephesians 3:15). The Bible tells the story of God. The Bible reveals God by describing His actions in history and His developing relationship to His creation.

Furthermore, God alone has the distinction of being without beginning, without origin. No other being in the universe exists in the same radical independence as the God of the Bible does. No other being is self-existent, self-explanatory, or self-sustaining. Naturally, this implies that before creation, all that existed was God. Many people, therefore, wonder what God was doing before He created the world and the people who live on it. Was He bored? Was He lonely? Did He create out of a need for something to do and someone to be with?

No. God was not bored. He did not create us for His amusement. Nor was He lonely. He did not create us to fulfill His need for fellowship. The Bible asserts that God is actually a communion of three persons who have loved each other and related to each other in perfect harmony for all eternity. For example, the Bible begins by saying, "In the beginning, God created the heavens and the earth. Now the earth had been unformed and uninhabitable and darkness blanketed the surface of the watery depths while the Spirit of God hovered over the water" (Genesis 1:1–2, author's translation). God and the Spirit were together in the beginning. They cooperated in creation.

Later the Gospel of John tells us about a third co-creator to this picture. John says,

In the beginning was the Word and the Word was inti-mately associated with God and the Word was himself divine. This Word existed in the beginning in intimate communion with God. All things were made through him and apart from him nothing was made that has been made (John 1:1–4, author's translation).

John identifies this Word with Jesus Christ (John 1:14) whom Paul says "is preeminent over all creation because by him everything was made" (Colossians 1:16, author's translation).

Thus, the Bible paints a picture of three persons who are one God, all of whom share the same radically indepen-dent existence while being united in an eternal, perfect relationship of pure, selfless love. These three persons, whom the Bible identifies as the Father, Son, and Spirit cooperated in creating all that exists. God is a communion of three persons who enjoyed each others' perfect compan-ionship so much that they decided to create a world with which to share the joys of perfect communion. 1 John 1:3–4 states it this way:

What we have seen and heard we declare also to you so that you can have a relationship with us and our relation-ship is with the Father and with His son Jesus Christ. We are telling you these things so that we can all be full of joy (author's translation).

These three persons, however, are not three gods. Their relationship is far too close to be described in terms of three separate gods. They are three persons who are so closely related and so perfectly united as to be one God. An important implication of the fact that God is a communion of three persons who have no beginning or origin is that love has no beginning or origin. Love has always existed. Community has always existed. Love and fellowship are the foundation of all reality as expressed in the relationship of the three persons who are one God and who created all things out of love and for love. No doubt this is what the Bible means when it says that God is love (1 John 4:8) and that love always has existed and always will exist (1 Corinthians 13:8).

So, God created not out of any selfish need for amusement or companionship. God is independent of His creation even for these necessities because God is himself a communion of three persons who are completely satisfied in each other's love. God's love, however, overflowed and created a world that could share God's joy in this perfect love.

This brings us back to God's story. God's story in the Bible begins not with God's origin but with ours. The God who has no beginning grants us a beginning, a meaningful and purposeful beginning. Unlike many of the world's creation stories in which humanity is an accident or an afterthought—the unintended result of a war between the gods or the unwanted offspring of a divine affair, the Bible's creation story reveals a god who creates with purpose. To emphasize this point, the Bible records how God, just before creating humankind, deliberates over how and why he will create humankind. The Father, Son, and Spirit enter divine consultation as they decide to make a special creature who will share a special relationship with them because, unlike the other animals, humans will bear God's own image. They will bear the solemn responsibility of ruling creation on God's behalf and reflecting in their relationships with each other the perfect unity and loving cooperation of the Father, Son, and Spirit.

> Then God said, "Let's make humankind in our own image, according to our own likeness so that they can govern the fish in the sea, the birds of the air, the beasts of the field, and all the crawling creatures that crawl upon the ground." So God created humankind in his own image, in the image of God he created him, male and female he created them (Genesis 1:26–27, author's translation).

Within a single paragraph the Bible states three times that humankind is created in the image of the one who is not created. Though we are not divine and never will be, we have a dignity that can come only from a God who has no beginning, no origin. He created us to reflect and exercise His loving dominion over all the earth and He meant to do it. He thought through the kind of relationship He wanted to have with us and the kind of role He wanted us to play in His world. Then He made us according to His plan.

The fact that God has no beginning, no origin or genealogy means that His existence is radically independent of anything or anyone outside of Himself. The fact of this independence and self-sufficiency means that God is free to love us and all of His creation selflessly, for no other reason than the sheer joy of loving and being loved in return. God has no beginning and no end; therefore, pure selfless love has no beginning and no end. Best of all, we as humans created in the image of the one who was not created get to be both the objects and channels of God's pure, selfless love. God expresses His pure, selfless love to the world through those who have surrendered themselves to Him, have all of their needs met by Him, and therefore can love as freely and selflessly as the God who was not created.

How this exciting and glorious possibility came about, however, is not as simple as it sounds. The human creatures God created in His own image rebelled against God and declared their independence from the only one who is truly independent. Humans thought that they could have a life separate and apart from God. Thus we severed our ties with God and in doing so severed our ties with our point of origin, our ancestry, our creator. This sad story is told about in Genesis 1–11. As a result, we have forgotten who we are. Our severance from our origins has created a terrible identity crisis and we have forgotten that we are the dependent image of the radically independent God. We have forgotten that we are designed to reflect, in a creaturely way, the pure, selfless love of the one who is not a creature, who has no beginning and no end.

Worse than that, we lost our ability to relate to God at all. It used to be difficult for dependent creatures with a defining origin to relate to a radically independent God with no origin at all. Now that we have rebelled, it is impossible, at least from our end.

Apart from God and his love, humans could do nothing but spiral downward into deeper selfishness, sin, and violence, hurling themselves headlong toward selfdestruction. Yet, as distorted and twisted as the creaturely image of the loving creator became, it was never destroyed. So the God who is not a creature decided to restore in His creatures the perfect image of God, a reflection of His pure, selfless love. Since relating to the God who has no beginning was impossible from our end, God made the first move. He restored us to knowledge of Himself, to relationship with Himself, and to our true identity as the creaturely image of the God who was not created.

He did this in a most mysterious, marvelous, and unexpected way. God injected himself into humanity. The God who has no beginning, no genealogy, no birth chose to be born as a human. He chose to have ancestry, a human beginning, a genealogy. Since we had always struggled to relate to a person without beginning or origin, God chose to have a beginning so that we could know Him again. He became human to remind us that to be human is to reflect the image of the God who has no beginning and to mediate the love that has always existed and always will exist. One of the three persons who share the divinity, the radical independence of the one God, became a dependent human. He depended on His human mother for nourishment, on His human father for shelter and clothes, and on His heavenly Father for the strength to be truly human, the creaturely image of the God who is not a creature.

The God who has no origin, no ancestry can now be known through the man, Jesus Christ: a man of Jewish origin, a man whose ancestry is the royal line of King David of the tribe of Judah, a man who was born in Bethlehem and grew up in Nazareth. More mysterious and marvelous still is that the God who has no end also chose to experience our end, the human end of death we had brought on ourselves by separating from God. He chose to die. He died so that we could be restored to the God we had abandoned, reconnected to our ultimate point of origin, reminded of our identity as the creaturely image of the God who has no beginning.

By becoming a dependent human, Jesus made a way for dependent humans to know the radically independent God. Jesus has reconciled humans whose end is death to a God whose life has no end. Jesus's human origin and human end, however, did not change the fact that He is the God without beginning and without end. He arose from the grave alive again as both God without beginning or end, and as man, with beginning but now without end. He made it possible for us to share in the very life of the eternal God. This resurrection was not to an endless cycle of death and rebirth, but to a never ending life and a pennanent victory over death. Otherwise, God would have numerous beginnings and endings as would we, trapped together in a revolving door of death and rebirth.

The God of the Bible, however, has no beginning and no end. His only birth is the birth that Jesus chose before He was human, so that as a human, He could reconcile humans to God. His only death is the human death He chose to die in order to conquer death. Jesus made it clear that His human birth was not the beginning of His existence in John 8:58 when He said to a group of fellow Jews, "Before our ancestor, Abraham, existed, I existed as the great I AM." He also made it clear that His human death would not be the end of His existence when He said in John 10:17–18,

> I lay down my life that I may take it up again. No one takes it from me, but I lay it down of my own accord. I have authority to lay it down, and I have authority to take it up again.

The remarkable thing is that because of Jesus's resurrection, death does not have to be our end either. We can share in the eternal life of Father, Son, and Spirit if we will accept God's offer of a relationship with Him.

It is truly difficult to relate to a person with no origin. However, because God underwent a human origin through the virgin birth of Jesus, we can know this God who has no beginning. In fact, this is the only way we can know Him. Jesus stated in Matthew 11:27, "No one knows the Son except the Father and no one knows the Father except the Son *and anyone to whom the Son chooses to reveal Him*" (emphasis added). Until we know this God we cannot truly know ourselves, for we were created in His image and He is the key to our identity as well as to our origin.

Questions for Thought and Discussion

1. Why is it so important for us to know where we came from?
2. What is the significance of God's assertion that His name is "I AM"? (Exodus 3:14)

3. Why did God choose to create a creature made in His image?
4. At what point did humans lose the ability to relate to a God with no origin? Do we still struggle to relate to Him today?
5. How did Jesus change the way we relate to God?

I AM a Person

Charles R. Webb

Relationships with other people are among the most treasured human experiences. Most people can think of one or more relationships with individuals that they cherish. It may be a relationship with a grandmother or grandfather, with a parent or both of our parents, with a brother or sister, or with a special friend. Whoever the person or persons may be, this relationship has made life richer, fuller, and more meaningful. Without the joy of meaningful relationships, we would be lonely and miserable people. We may enjoy a hobby, such as fishing, or we may like our house, but we can only have a real relationship with another person. We cannot establish an emotionally meaningful, reciprocal relationship with inanimate objects such as an automobile, a piece of land, or a house.

The great news of the Bible is that God is essentially personal. The Bible makes it clear that God is a person, always has been a person, and will always be a person. God is not presented to us in the Bible as an eternal force or a perfect state of existence. Rather, God is personal, which means that humans can have a meaningful, personal relationship with God. If God were only a force or state of existence, people would be left to their own power and devices to grow spiritually. As a person, however, God can enter into a personal relationship with each of us and provide us support and strength in our spiritual development. Since God is a person, personhood is not something that we try to escape from through spiritual development; rather, personhood is the ultimate truth about God and humans.

It is true that just because God is a person does not automatically mean that we can have a personal relationship with Him. For example, the ruler of a foreign nation is a person, but it does not mean that we can have a personal relationship with that ruler just because he or she is a person. We can have a healthy personal relationship with a person only if both parties desire such a relationship. Jesus, God in the flesh, made it clear that God desires a healthy relationship with humans based on love and that He wants us to have a healthy relationship with Him based on love. He was once asked which was the most important commandment.

> The most important one, answered Jesus, is this: ... "Love the Lord your God with all your heart and with all your soul and with all your mind and with all your strength." The second is this: "Love your neighbor as yourself." There is no commandment greater than these (Mark 12:28–31).

These verses capture beautifully the desire of both parties. First, God desires a relationship with us. Jesus goes so far as to state that this is the most important command of the Bible. Second, God wants us to desire and seek a loving relationship, not only with Him, but with other people.

We can desire and have a faith-based, loving relationship with God because He is a person. God can be described as a person because personhood does not refer to the nature of a person. The characteristics of personhood, which will be discussed shortly, can apply to either a divine or a human person. Before we look at the Biblical view of God's personhood, the distinction between the personhood of God and personhood of humans must be clarified. The fact that God is a person and human beings are persons does not mean that God and people are the same in their personhood. God is always God, and we are always His creation. It is true that God is eternal and exists in a perfect, loving relationship as the Father, Son, and Holy Spirit. God is personhood wrapped in the qualities of the infinite creator of all things, and we are persons wrapped in the finite qualities that define a human being. God, as a person, does not share in any way the frailties and moral failures associated with human beings as persons.

It is also true that God transcends the physical aspects of human personhood such as maleness or femaleness, skin color, and other features that physically differentiate one human from another human. The pronouns used to refer to God in the Bible are intended to emphasize the personhood of God, not necessarily His maleness. Although the masculine pronoun is used when referring to God, it does not mean that God is a male in the human sense of having a male body form. God is a spiritual being, not physical (John 4:24).

Personhood is defined in various ways depending on the purpose of the definition. For example, a legal definition includes elements of personhood that are distinctive to on the legal situation. But all definitions include some common or core elements of what we mean when we refer to personhood. These common aspects of the definition of personhood include: (1) volition of attention and action;(2) self-awareness; (3) memory and history, and (4) the ability to enter into and establish relationships with other persons (I will define these terms in the next few paragraphs). The Bible makes it abundantly clear that God possesses all of the elements of personhood listed above. It is interesting to note that the definition of personhood does not include any elements that limits personhood to the finite situation that we presently inhabit. And likewise, God, an infinite person, is in no way limited in His deity by the fact of His personhood.

That God is a person is taught emphatically throughout the Bible. But we have to read only the first few chapters of the Bible to understand that God possesses all of the characteristics of personhood that are listed above, as can be seen in the following brief discussion of each element of the definition.

First, *volition of attention and action* simply refers to the fact that a person has the freedom to selectively direct his attention to certain objects and the freedom to choose whether to perform certain actions. In Genesis 4:6–7, God directs His attention to a specific person, Cain. "Then the Lord said to Cain, 'Why are you angry? Why is your face downcast? If you do what is right, will you not be accepted?'" In Genesis 1:26, God chooses to perform a specific act.

> Then God said, "Let us make man in our image and in our likeness and let them rule over the fish of the sea and the birds of the air, over the livestock, over all the earth, and over all creatures that move along the ground."

These verses are only two of the many references that could be cited in the first chapters of Genesis that refer to God's freedom to attend selectively and God's freedom to act.

Second, *self-awareness* means that one is aware of his existence and that he exists apart from other persons. In Genesis 6:18, God says, "But I will establish my covenant with you, and you will enter the ark—you and your wife and your sons and your sons' wives with you." Here God distinguishes Himself from another person, Noah when he asks Noah to enter onto an ark. This passage, along with the numerous other passages in which God refers to himself as "I", leaves no doubt of God's self-awareness.

Third, *memory and history* refer to the fact that a person remembers things that have happened in the past; in other words, a person is aware of his existence before the present time. Genesis 6:6 says, "The Lord was grieved that He had made man on the earth and His heart was filled with pain." In this passage, God remembers having created man, and He experiences emotions. Though experiencing emotions is not one of the primary characteristics of personhood, it is a clear indicator of personhood.

Fourth, the *ability to have relationships with other persons* refers to the ability to experience all the changes and adjustments that relationships entail. From a human perspective, the relational aspect of God's personhood is the most meaningful. Therefore, I will spend most of this chapter dealing with what the Bible tells us about the relationship between God and humans. Chapters 1–6 in Genesis illustrate that a relationship existed between God and humans from the time God created humans. Genesis 3 describes how the loving, healthy relationship between God and humanity was broken by sin. Chapters 4–5 show the downward spiral of that broken relationship until God sent a flood of water to destroy the earth in chapter 6. Looking at it from another perspective, Cain kills his brother Abel (chapter 3)—showing us that a broken relationship with God results in broken relationships with each other. Finally, chapters 6–7 show how this broken relationship with each other leads to mass violence and human estrangement The level of wickedness reaches such a level that it becomes necessary for God to bring all of the evil to an end. He sends a flood to purge the world of evil and provide a fresh start.

After the flood, humans, sensing their alienation from God and inability to successfully relate to each other, take matters into their own hands and try to resume relationships by their own means. This condition culminates with the tower of Babel. The description of the city with a tower in Babel is found in Genesis 11, and it demonstrates the confusion that results when people try, without the help of God, (1) to determine their own course in life and (2) to restore their relationships with other humans and with God. The story also makes clear that the relationship between God and humans is so broken that it requires more than just healing. It requires a new relationship through a new means. The story of this new relationship begins in Genesis chapter twelve.

Throughout the first eleven chapters of Genesis, God has been seeking a relationship with humans. This is not because God somehow needs relationship with humans but simply because He wants relationship with humans. Humans, on the other hand, do need a relationship with God. Thus, God seeks a relationship with humans because we need it and He wants it. The Bible is then essentially the story of God's pursuit of healthy relationships with His human creatures starting with Abraham and his descendants, who grow into a nation that He chooses as His own special people and then, through them, eventually with the entire world.

In chapter 12 of Genesis, God takes the initiative in this new relationship and reaches out to Abraham. Abraham was not seeking God; rather, God was seeking him. God removes Abraham from his familiar surroundings to encourage his dependence on Him, and so that he might focus on this new foundational relationship with God. This move, in Abraham's case, involved physical relocation. More importantly, however, God today seeks to deliver us from our old life of broken relationships and fruitless activity into a new life of fellowship and productivity.

What Abraham leaves behind is his inheritance. As his father's eldest, he would have received his father's land and home. Abraham forsakes this in order to pursue a new inheritance—a faith relationship with God. However, he takes along his own possessions, his wife, his slaves, and any relatives who desire to walk the road of faith with him. Today we can have the same faith relationship, characterized by the love that Abraham had with God. God wants us to take our possessions and relatives into this relationship with Him, just as Abraham took these things with him into his relationship with God.

In the story of God's call of Abraham, God is portrayed as one who makes and keeps promises. He promises Abraham a new home (a new land), children from whom many nations will be born, a great and important name and reputation, and the opportunity to be a blessing to everyone in the world. This will only occur, however, if Abraham trusts that God can and will do all of this for him. That trust manifests itself in Abraham's obedience and willingness to follow God into the unknown.

Just as in Abraham's case, our relationship with God inspires greater and greater obedience. As Jesus said, "If you love Me you will keep my coImnandments" (John 8:32). But our relationship with God is not based on the quality of our obedience. A genuine relationship with God produces quality obedience, but quality obedience does not produce a genuine relationship with God. We can obey a command out of fear, or for some other reason, without any feeling of love or a desire for a healthy loving relationship with the person giving the command. For example, a person in the military may obey all the commands of a superior officer while having a strong dislike for that officer. But unlike what many humans would do, God does not end His relationship with Abraham when Abraham stumbles in his faith. He loves him through it, The biblical story is a story of love from beginning to end. The biblical story of love is the story of the heart of God, the heart of a person. In the Bible, we see the heart of God on display. We see the great desire that God has for a relationship with humans, because He created us in His image and He knows how much we need Him. We see the great lengths to which God has gone to initiate and maintain a relationship with people. God does this despite the fact that people have often rejected Him and have been untrue to Him because they do not realize how much they need Him.

In the story of Hosea and Gomer (which in reality is the story of God and His people), we see Hosea again and again go in search of his wife despite her unfaithfulness. When relating the story of God and His people, Nehemiah made the following incredible statement:

> They became stiff-necked ... but you are a forgiving God, gracious and compassionate, slow to anger and abounding in love. Therefore you did not desert them; stubbornly they turned their backs on you ... but in your great mercy you did not put an end to them or abandon them, for you are a gracious and merciful God; in your compassion you delivered them time after time. (Nehemiah 9:17, 31, 28)

Because God is a loving person, He is able to have a loving relationship with His creation. A second implication of God's personhood can be drawn from this understanding of the God-human relationship. Because God loves, He can be hurt by those He loves just as any other person can. The Old Testament especially develops the concept of the suffering of God that is brought about by various activities of man. God suffers because people reject Him as their God. God suffers because the people reject a relationship with Him or they have broken their relationship with Him. Just before God destroyed most of humanity in the flood, the Bible says, "The Lord was grieved that He made man on the earth, and His heart was filled with pain" (Genesis 6:6). God's heart was filled with pain because of the way in which people had broken their relationship with Him and rejected Him to pursue their own selfish directions.

In addition to God suffering because of people, God suffers with people. Because of the great compassion of God for humankind, He suffers when we are suffering. Third, God suffers for people. He suffers when we make bad decisions, for He knows how much we will suffer and how much suffering we will cause others because of the bad decisions we make. Without God's help, humans will often make decisions that lead to their own destruction, as well as to the destruction of their families and loved ones. "I know, God, that mere mortals can't run their own lives; that men and women don't have what it takes to take charge of life" (Jeremiah 10:23).

The ultimate expression of the suffering of God is when He allowed His son, Jesus, to die crucified upon a cross. In this case, crucifixion was the nailing or hanging of a human on a wooden cross, a form of capital punishment reserved for executing criminals. God allowed His son to die a criminal's death! He did this and suffered because of and for the sins of all people. On the cross God suffered more than we suffer; in fact, when we suffer, God always suffers more than we do, as any good father would. God would be a god without integrity if He loves us as much as He indicated that He does throughout the Bible, yet did not suffer because for, and with us. It is simply impossible to divorce oneself motionally from a person or people that one loves deeply and desires an intimate relationship with.

In this short chapter, the personhood of God and its implications for humans have been explored. Other implications could be drawn from the fact that God is a person. For example, because God is person, He is knowable as any other person is knowable. Clearly because God is divine, humans can never thoroughly know or understand God, but He is knowable to the extent that He has revealed himself to us.

Because God is a person and we are persons, we can in a significant measure identify with God. But God in His wisdom gives us more than just written instructions to help us to understand Him and identify with Him. He knew that we needed a living example that we could identify with, so He sent His Son in the form of a man. In the flesh, Jesus (God) experienced what we experience as humans. This was not because He did not know what it was like to be a human, but He did it for our benefit. It is much easier for us to identify with God in the flesh than God in heaven.

For we do not have a high priest who is unable to sympathize with our weaknesses, but we have one who has

been tempted in every way, just as we are—yet was without sin. Let us then approach the throne of grace with confidence, so that we may receive mercy and find grace to help us in our time of need (Hebrews 4:15–16).

Questions for Thought and Discussion

1. How does the fact that God is a person, as opposed to a force or a feeling, affect us as humans?
2. What are some similarities and differences between God's personhood and ours?
3. Does God's personhood mean that He is limited in some way? Why or why not?
4. What examples from Abraham's life illustrate God's personhood?
5. How are God's personhood, love, and suffering interconnected?

I AM Triune

David H. Warren

The term "Godhead" (actually an archaic spelling for "Godhood") refers to the concept that God exists in the form of three persons. Another expression for this concept is the word "Trinity." Our English word "Trinity" comes from the Latin word for "three."

While many Christians believe in the concept of the Godhead or the Trinity, the honest student of the Bible must confess that this doctrine is not explicitly or expressly taught anywhere in the Scriptures. No biblical writer ever discusses it, and no biblical passage ever uses the terms "Godhead" or "Trinity" in referring to the nature of God. In fact, neither term is ever used anywhere in the Bible.

The Term "Godhead"

The term "Godhead" does actually appear three times in the old English translation of the Bible known as the "King James Version" or "Authorized Version" of 1611. In the King James Version at Acts 17:29, the apostle Paul stands before the Epicurean and Stoic philosophers in Athens and declares: "Forasmuch then as we are the offspring of God, we ought not to think that the Godhead is like unto gold, or silver, or stone, graven by art and man's device." And again in Romans 1:20, the same inspired writer assures his Roman readers: "For the invisible things of him from the creation of the world are clearly seen, being understood by the things that are made, even his eternal power and Godhead; so that they are without excuse." And finally in Colossians 2:9 as it is rendered in the old, venerable King James Version, Paul, in writing about the "Christ" (vs. 8), emphatically affirms: "For in him dwelleth all the fullness of the Godhead bodily."

But contrary to the wording of the King James Version, none of these passages is actually talking about the "Godhead" or the "Trinity" as a reference to the tripartite nature God. Since the New Testament portion of the Bible was originally inspired and written in the ancient Greek language, anyone wanting to know precisely the meaning of a biblical term or phrase in this portion of the Bible must consider carefully what the Greek language really means. And in none of these three passages does the Greek actually refer to the "Godhead" or the "Trinity" as the tripartite nature of God. Instead these Greek words are referring to the concept of "deity," or the "divinity," or the "divine nature" of God.

Now it is true that in each of these three passages, Paul uses a different Greek word. But in each instance, the Greek word that Paul uses merely refers to the "divine nature" or "divinity" of God. In none of these three passages does Paul actually affirm that God has a tripartite nature. Instead, each of these three Greek words is related to the other two, just as in English "divine nature" is related etymologically to "divinity." But none of them refers to the concept of the "Godhead" or the "Trinity."

For this reason, more modern English translations of the Bible use terms like "Deity" (Revised Standard Version, first published in 1946) or "Divine Nature" (New American Standard Bible, first published in 1963, and the New King James Version, first published in 1979) instead of "God-head" in the wording of Acts 17:29, Romans 1:20, and Colossians 2:9. So the term "Godhead" is only found in older translations of the Bible like the King James Version. But in actuality, the term never really occurs in the Greek Bible.

The Term "Trinity"

Likewise, the term "Trinity" never occurs in the Bible. The English term "Trinity" comes from Latin and is derived from the Latin adjective trini meaning "three" or "three-fold." The word "Trinity" as used of God was forged in the heat of the many controversies surrounding the nature of Christ that sprang up when the Roman Empire officially stopped persecuting Christians in A.D. 313. There were, unfortunately, differences in beliefs among Christians before this date, but the threat of persecution kept these differences in check. As long as the Roman Empire was persecuting Christians, Christians were less inclined to fight among themselves.

But peace and prosperity finally came to the church with Constantine, the first "Christian" emperor of Rome. In time Constantine made Christianity the state religion of the empire. With no more enemies from without to hold it together, Christianity began to break apart from the internal fissures created by the Christians themselves due to their differences over the nature of Christ and His relationship to God.

In an effort to restore peace within the church, the emperor began the practice of holding a general church council and inviting representatives from every segment of the empire. He pressured all of the participants to agree on a "creed" or official statement of their beliefs. But such creeds only served to deepen the lines of division, thus calling forth another council. In the many ecumenical church councils that followed, the term "Trinity" became an important word for those who claimed to represent the orthodox position of the Bible. God, they explained, exists in three distinct persons.

Thus, the terms "Godhead" and "Trinity" are never actually found in the Bible. They came to be used by Christians in an effort to formulate their own understandings of the biblical concept of God. But the Bible never explicitly teaches a doctrine of the Godhead or the Trinity.

But Is the Godhead Taught Implicitly in the Bible?

Since the terms "Godhead" and "Trinity" are not found in the Bible, many modern scholars have concluded that it is a doctrine not found in the Bible. For example, in *The New Encyclopcedia Britannica*, one can read:

> Neither the word Trinity nor the explicit doctrine appears in the New Testament, nor did Jesus and his followers intend to contradict the Shema in the Old Testament: "Hear, o Israel: The Lord our God is one Lord" (Deuteronomy 6:4). ...
>
> The doctrine developed gradually over several centuries and through many controversies .... by the end of the 4th century ... the doctrine of the Trinity took substantially the fonn it has maintained ever since [*Micropcedia*, vol. 11 (1991), p. 928].

One can find a similar statement in *The Encyclopedia Americana* that seems to go even further in denying that the doctrine of the Trinity is taught in the Bible:

> Christianity derived from Judaism and Judaism was strictly Unitarian [believing that God is one person]. The road which led from Jerusalem to Nicea was scarcely a straight one. Fourth century Trinitarianism did not reflect accurately early Christian teaching regarding the nature of God; it was, on the contrary, a deviation from this teaching [vol. 27 (1956), p. 294L].

More startling is this statement from Yale University professor E. Washburn Hopkins:

> To Jesus and Paul the doctrine of the trinity was apparently unknown; at any rate, they say nothing about it [*Origin and Evolution of Religion* (New Haven, CT: Yale University Press, 1923): 336].

Perhaps Paul did not fully understand everything that he wrote by inspiration. But even Jesus did not know about the doctrine of the Trinity? Such statements like this one deny the divinity of Christ. He who knew the very thoughts of every man (Mark 2:8; John 2:24–25) also knew where he came from and who he was (John 17:5). Surely Jesus himself knew whether there was a Trinity or not!

Many liberal theologians and scholars today with a low opinion of the Bible and its divine origin believe that the church of the fourth century *invented* the doctrine of the Trinity. But the early church did not create this doctrine. We must be careful to distinguish between the creation of a doctrine and the *recognition* of a doctrine. And we must also be careful to distinguish between that which is explicitly taught in Scripture and that which is implicitly taught in Scripture.

Even Jesus himself was careful to recognize that whatever is implied in Scripture is just as true as that which is expressly stated. For example, in his debate with the Sadducees on the Tuesday before his death, Jesus proved the resurrection of the dead from a clear implication of a biblical statement. When the Sadducees, who denied the bodily resurrection, challenged Jesus, he replied: "Now concerning the resurrection of the dead, have you not read the statement spoken to you by God, 'I am the God of Abraham, and the God of Isaac, and the God of Jacob'? He is not the God of the dead but of the living" (Matthew 22:31–32; compare Mark 12:26–27 and Luke 20:37–38). Jesus here is quoting Exodus 3:6, where God is speaking to Moses from the burning bush. Jesus cites this statement as proof that Abraham, Isaac, and Jacob still exist somewhere, even though they have been dead by the time of Moses for many centuries. Like the Jehovah's Witnesses today, the Sadducees believed that a person's soul does not survive death. Jesus, on the other hand, taught that a person's soul does indeed survive death (Matthew 10:28) and that on the last day one's soul will be reunited with the body in the Great Resurrection (John 5:28–29; 11:23–26, 43–44; see also James 2:26).

Everything implied by biblical statements is just as true as the biblical statements themselves. Now it is possible for us humans to fail in recognizing an implication or to err in overstating its significance. But whatever is truly implied in the Bible is just as true as the Bible's bold declarations, for God has inspired both of them (2 Peter 1:21). In regard to the doctrine of the Trinity, I believe that it is found in the Bible but was not more fully understood until much later.

Statements in the Old Testament

The very first verse in the Bible teaches us that there is a plurality as well as a unity in the nature of God. In Genesis 1:1 we read, "In the beginning God created the heavens and the earth." In Hebrew, the word here for "God" (in Hebrew the word is *Elohim*) is a plural form, but the verb "created" is in the singular. Thus, the very first verse of the Bible tells us that there is something plural and yet curiously singular about the nature of God.

Later in this same chapter, we hear God say, "Let *us* make man in *our* image, according to *our* likeness" (Genesis 1:26). To whom was God here speaking? It was not to his angels, for the next verse clarifies that the possessive pronoun "our" actually refers only to "God." Genesis 1:27 states that "God created man in *His* image; in the *image of God* He created him. . . . " The text does not say that God made man in the image of Himself as well as in that of the angels. God made man only in *His* own image. Here again we see that there is something plural and yet curiously singular about the nature—the image—of God.

Again in Genesis 11:5–8, one reads where "the Lord" came down to see the Tower of Babel and says, "Come, let *Us*; go down and confuse their language" (vs. 7). And then in vs. 8, we read where "the Lord" scattered them over all the earth. Perhaps the pronoun "Us" here includes the Lord's angels, but there is no mention of His angels in this text. Sandwiched between references to "the Lord," this "Us" appears to be another reference to the plurality of God's nature.

Some students of the Bible also see a reference to this plurality of God in Isaiah 6:8, "Whom shall *I* send? And who will go for *Us*?" Here again we find the singular ("I") juxtaposed with the plural ("Us"). There are those who would argue that this "Us" includes divine beings or perhaps even God's angels. Admittedly the reference here to the plural is less clear, as in the previous instance. Nevertheless, when taken together, all these passages seem to affirm that there is some sort of "plurality" in the nature of God.

But There Can Only Be One God

And yet there are clear statements in the Bible that declare that there is only one God. For example, the singularity of God is unmistakably affirmed, when God declares: "Hear, O Israel! The Lord is our God; the Lord is one" (Deuteronomy 6:4). And again one reads in the prophet Isaiah, "I am the Lord, and there is no other. Besides me there is no God" (Isaiah 45:5). And finally there is this brief but clear statement from the Apostle Paul: "There is no God but one" (1 Corinthians 8:4).

So how can there be "three" when there is only "one" God? This is precisely where many people, like the Muslims, believe that the concept of "one God" (*Quran* 3:2, 62)rules out any notion of a Trinity (*Quran* 4:171; 5:73; 6:19). Even within some branches of Christendom, there are groups like the Jehovah's Witnesses who deny the doctrine of the Trinity.

But does a divine truth become negated simply because it extends beyond the limits of human understanding? Why should we humans with our limited capacity for knowledge expect to fathom all the mysteries of a limitless God and His nature? Should we be surprised to learn that there are some aspects of the nature of Almighty God that are so great that they surpass our limited capability to grasp them? Even in his own treatise on the doctrine of the

Trinity, Augustine of Hippo felt compelled to admit, "I ... confess that the wonderful knowledge of Him is too great for me, and that I cannot attain to it" (*On the Trinity* 15.27.50).

Several years ago in a college class, I witnessed a helpful illustration of how there can be three entities, and yet at the same time from another perspective there is only one entity. Using a transparency projector, my professor projected onto a screen the image of a circle. "How many circles do you see?" he asked the class. Only one circle was visible. And so we students all answered in unison, "One!" Then the professor took his finger and moved the top transparency sheet just a few inches over. "Now," he asked, "how many circles do you see?" There were now two circles visible on the screen. And so we all answered together again, "Two!" He then took his finger once more and moved the second transparency that was beneath the upper one, so that now three distinct circles were being projected onto the screen. "How many circles do you see now?" We all responded together, "Three!"

At this point several of us students began to realize that our professor had lying on his projector three clear transparency sheets, and on each of these transparency sheets there was a single circle. The professor then picked up these three transparency sheets. Aligning them once again in his hands, he gently tapped the bottom edge of the three-layered stack of transparency sheets on the top surface of the projector and then laid them down flat on the surface of the projector. "So how many circles do you see now?"

Only one circle was now visible on the screen. Yet all of

us knew that there were actually three separate transparency sheets lying on the surface of the projector, on stacked on top of another. And since each transparency sheet had a circle on it, we knew that there should be three circles. But only one was visible. Why? Only one circle was visible now because all three circles again had the same center point and the same radius. With the same center point and the same radius, the three circles on the transparency sheets appeared to be only one circle on the screen. But actually we all knew that there were three circles lying on top of each other.

We humans are all different. No two of us are exactly alike. Some of us are short, while others of us are tall. Some are thin, while others are fat. Our differences represent various degrees of limitation. But can you imagine a level of being where all of the individuals are exactly alike in every conceivable respect? None of them has any limitations. All of them are perfect in every characteristic. They are all identical. Each of them is completely good and holy. There can be no subtle differences among them in regard to their essence or to any characteristic, for any single difference from their perfect state would result in an imperfection in one of them. Just as the three circles with the same exact measurements appeared as one circle, in a similar way three individuals at the level of being which we call "God," each having the same exact characteristics and the same exact essence as the other two, would appear as one: One God, but three separate persons.

Statements in the New Testament

Admittedly, the concept of one God but three separate persons is difficult, if not impossible, for us humans to grasp. Admittedly, such a concept is never mentioned *explicitly* in the Bible. However, there are some passages in the New Testament where this concept does seem to be taken for granted. In other words, it appears to be implied. And this concept of the Godhead or the Trinity also seems to be implied, if we take seriously certain statements in the New Testament made about Jesus Christ and His relationship to God.

There are statements in the New Testament where the concept of the Godhead or Trinity is clearly implied. The first such statement is the "Great Commission" according to the Gospel of Matthew. Just before He left the earth (usually called "The Ascension" by Christians), Jesus issued this final charge to His apostles: "Therefore go and make disciples of all nations, baptizing them in the name of the Father and of the Son and of the Holy Spirit, teaching them to obey everything that I have commanded you" (Matthew 28:19–20a). Here we find the Father, the Son, and the Holy Spirit in parallel, a situation which would seem to make them equal to each other in some sense. The phrase "in the name of" probably means "by the authority of," the use of the singular "name" here suggesting that they stand equal in authority to each other and perhaps even have the same authority.

Another statement is the apostle Paul's closing wish to the church in the city of Corinth: "May the grace of the Lord Jesus Christ, and the love of God, and the fellowship of the Holy Spirit be with you all" (2 Corinthians 13:14). Paul's bracketing "God" here with "the Lord Jesus Christ" on one side and with "the Holy Spirit" on the other would seem to imply that these three divine persons are all three on the same level. If "God" in this verse refers to "the Father," then we have here another reference to the Father the Son, Holy Spirit. This passage explains that each of these divine persons shows a particular aspect of God toward humans. The Son shows us grace through His vicarious death for the sins of all humanity (John 1:15–17, 29). The Spirit embraces us in fellowship when He indwells in us, once our sins have been taken away (Acts 2:38; Romans 8:9). But it is God the Father from whom we receive love, (1 John 3:1), for all "love comes from God" (4:7). These distinctive roles for each person in the Godhead will be explained later when we consider the tripartite nature of man (see the final section below).

One can also find traces of the divine trio in Ephesians 2:18 and 1 Peter 1:2. In all of these passages, references to "the Son" or Jesus and to "the Spirit" or "the Holy Spirit" are placed on the same level with the references to "God" or "the Father." In none of these instances is their relationship to each other explained. It is merely assumed. It is as if God does not feel the need to explain Himself fully to humans. When we reach these limits of the text, all we can do is respect God and the limits to how He has revealed Himself to us.

Jesus As Deity

The biblical concept of the Godhead or the Trinity includes the nature of Jesus Christ's relationship to God. Unlike the doctrine of the Godhead or the Trinity, which is not taught explicitly in the Bible, the doctrine that "Jesus is God" is taught explicitly in the Bible. The clearest statement of this truth is found in John 1:1, "And the Word was God."

There are several other passages in both the Old Testament and the New Testament that teach that Jesus is God. Jesus is clearly called "Mighty God" in Isaiah 9:6. In John 12:41, the apostle John comments that the prophet Isaiah saw "his glory and spoke of him," referring to Isaiah's vision of God in Isaiah 6:1–5, 10, which the apostle John quotes in John 12:40. The only possible antecedent of John's "his" and "him" in John 12:41 is Jesus (vs. 36–37) Mattew 1:23 (quoting Isaiah 7:14) states that Jesus was "God with us." In what sense was Jesus on earth "God with us"? Clearly this phrase implies that Jesus is God, so that when Jesus was with us humans, one could also say that "God is with us."

According to John 5:18, the Jews understood that when Jesus said that God was His father, He was "making Himself equal with God." In John 10:33, the Jews accused Jesus of blasphemy because He "claimed to be God." The apostle Thomas calls Jesus "My Lord and my God" in John 20:28. Apparently Jesus accepted this identification in verse 29, since he does not correct Thomas here. The apostle Paul calls Jesus "our great God and Savior, Jesus Christ" (Titus 2:13). Revelation 1:17 refers to Jesus as "the first and the last," a phrase which in the Old Testament is reserved only for God Himself (Isaiah 41:4; 44:6; 48:12). How can you have two firsts? two lasts? Surely this phrase shows that Jesus is God!

Man's Reflection of God's Image

Why do the Scriptures teach explicitly that Jesus is God, and yet only teach the tripartite nature of God implicitly? Perhaps we should not try to answer questions that the Bible itself does not answer. Rather we should be content simply to consider and eventually come to trust what the Bible does say. While the Bible never explicitly teaches about the Godhead or the Trinity, there are some passages that seem to imply that our singular God exists in a plurality of three: One God in Three Persons or entities.

One can even see this tripartite nature of God in humans. In 1 Thessalonians 5:23, the apostle Paul mentions that man has a body, a soul, and a spirit. While many believe that the soul and the spirit are synonymous, the Bible carefully distinguishes between them (Hebrews 4:12). The soul is the seat of one's emotions and desires, of one's appetites and cravings. Deuteronomy 23:24 says, "In case you go into the vineyard of your fellowman, you must eat only enough grapes for you to satisfy your soul, but you must not put any into a receptacle of yours." A more literal reading states, "You shall eat grapes according to your soul, your satisfaction" (Note that the last two terms are nouns and are synonymous). 2 Samuel 3:21 states, "You will certainly become king over all that your soul craves" (also 1 Kings 11:37). The Hebrew term for "soul" can even refer to animals, since they too have appetites and cravings ("living creatures," Genesis 1:20–21). It can even refer to the sex drive/cravings of a zebra in heat: Jeremiah 2:24, "A zebra accustomed to the wilderness, at the craving of her soul, snuffing up the wind; at her time for copulation, who can turn her back?" It can also refer to loftier or spiritual appetites and cravings, as in Psalm 42:1–2,

> As the hind that longs for the water streams, so my very soul longs for you, O God. My soul indeed thirsts for God, for the living God. When shall I go and see the face of God?

As the seat of one's emotions, the "soul" is the part of man that loves (Deuteronomy 30:6; Song of Solomon 1:7; 3: 1–4; Jeremiah 12:7), and rejoices (Psalm 86:4), and even weeps (1 Samuel 1:10). In contrast, the "spirit" is that part of man that reasons, thinks, and communicates with others (Exodus 28:3; Deuteronomy 34:9; Job 32:8, 18; Ezekiel 11:5b; 20:32; Mark 2:8; 1 Corinthians 2: 11).

Since humans were created in God's image (Genesis 1:26–27), we should not be surprised to find that the tripartite nature of God is mirrored in the human nature.

God	Human
Father	Soul
Son	Body
Holy Spirit	Spirit

In the Godhead, it is the Father that expresses emotion: "For God so loved the world that he gave his one and only Son ..." (John 3:16). "See how great the love which the Father has given to us ..." (1 John 3:1). In humans, it is the soul that expresses emotion. In the Godhead, it is the

Son that carries out actions: "All things were made through him, nothing was made without him" (John 1:3). "All things were created by him" (Colossians 1:16). It was the Son who came to earth and made atonement for sin. It was He who carried out the will of God on earth (Hebrews 10:5–7). In humans, it is the physical body that carries out the actions. In the Godhead, it is the Spirit that communicates (1 Timothy 4:1) and inspires people to speak prophetic messages (2 Peter 1:21). In humans, it is our spirit that reasons and communicates with others.

Conclusion

Since the concept of the Godhead or the Trinity is not taught anywhere explicitly in the Scriptures—no biblical writer ever discusses it, and even the very words "Godhead" or "Trinity" are not found anywhere in the Bible—perhaps we Christians should not make too much of it. It is a doctrine that many simply cannot understand, and it is surely one that none of us can fully fathom. However, I think it is a doctrine that is important for helping us understand the God of the Bible better.

Yet this doctrine is indeed implied in the Scriptures. And since everything implied in the Scriptures is just as true as everything explicitly taught in them, we must conclude that the doctrine of the Godhead or the Trinity is true. Perhaps we humans should find comfort—and even take pride—in the fact that at the very core of our being, we bear the unmistakable imprint of our God.

Questions for Thought and Discussion

1. What scriptures implicitly teach the doctrine of the Trinity?
2. How can the ideas of a singular God and a tripartite God both be accurate?
3. Does John 1 implicitly teach the doctrine of the Trinity? Why?
4. Does human nature reflect the triune nature of God? Why or why not?
5. Can a religion which rejects the idea of a tripartite God properly worship Him? Why or why not?

I AM Almighty

Wayne Barrier

A study of God reveals numerous attributes that place Him in the category of supernatural being. It is difficult for humans to comprehend the meaning of terms like eternal, infinite, spiritual, perfect, all-knowing, omniscient, perfectly just, all truthful, all powerful (omnipotent), and pure love. Humanity's concept and understanding of these attributes and traits is based on the limits of human intelligence and experiences. Humans can do great and powerful works using their knowledge of the natural world, but God can go beyond the human's limited being to do things that are not natural.

God's power can be understood on a limited basis by simply considering the force, energy, and intelligence needed to form the universe. This power is superior to anything any person has ever formed or created. God's power is not only greater than any other known force and energy source, but God's power is a controlled power. God created the heavens and the earth. Before these things existed, there was nothing. God's power is accompanied by superior knowledge, and the result of this combination of capacities resulted in the creation of life and the physical world as a sustainable system of life, matter, and energy. "God Almighty" is based on the Bible term, El Shaddai, which also means "God most High." This term is used in Genesis 17:1, which states, "And when Abram was ninety years old and nine, the LORD appeared to Abram and said unto him, 'I am the Almighty God, walk before me, and be thou perfect.'" This term is different from Elohim (see chapter 3), which is used to refer to the creator (Genesis 1). The term El Shaddai deals with the idea of going beyond creation and being involved in all natural processes to preserve man and the world for God's purposes. Yahweh and Jehovah are also names for God, each including the concept of an all-powerful being. To clarify this further, I will present a practical study of several considerations that define and demonstrate God's power by looking at the Bible, the sole authoritative source that provides information to help us understand God.

God the Creator

The Biblical account of creation is the most logical explanation of how the heavens and earth came into existence. Consider Genesis 1:1, which states, "In the beginning God created the heavens and the earth." This short statement describes an event that requires power beyond anything any person has ever possessed or can even comprehend. God did this. As we look further at the creation account in the Bible (Genesis 1 and 2), we read how God made everything including the sun, moon, earth, water, all life forms including man and woman, and put this creation in a sustainable state that continues to exist today. Humans cannot duplicate this process or event. Humans cannot make matter. Humans cannot create laws of nature found in physics, chemistry, biology, zoology, geology, astronomy, and botany.

The Bible is filled with references that acknowledge the creative power of God:

1 Chronicles 16:26 For all the gods of the people are idols; but the LORD made the heavens.

Nehemiah 9:6 Thou hast made heaven, the heaven of heavens, with all their host, the earth, and all the things that are therein, the seas, and all that is therein and thou preservest them all.

Job 5:8–10 But as for me, I would seek God, and to God I would commit my cause, who does great things, and unsearchable marvelous things without number. He gives rain on the earth and sends water on the fields.

Job 9:8 Which alone spreadeth out the heavens, and treadeth upon the waves of the sea. Which maketh Arcturus, Orion, and Pleiades, and the chambers of the south.

Psalms 8:3 When I consider thy heavens, the work of thy fingers, the moon and the stars which thou hast ordained … .

Psalms 19:1 The heavens declare the glory of God; and the firmament showeth his handiwork.

Psalms 33:6–9 By the word of the LORD were the heavens made; and all the host of them by the breath of his mouth. He gathered the waters of the sea together as an heap; he layeth up the depth in storehouses. For he spoke, and it was done; he commanded, and it stood fast.

Psalms 90:2 Before the mountains were brought forth, or ever You had formed the earth and the World, even from everlasting to everlasting, thou art God.

Psalms 124:8 Our help is in the name of the LORD, who made heaven and earth.

Isaiah 17:7 At that day shall a man look to his maker, and his eyes shall have respect to the Holy One of Israel.

Ecclesiastes 11:5 As thou knowest not what is the way of the spirit, nor how the bones do grow in the womb of her that is with child; even so thou knowest not the works of God, who maketh all.

Jeremiah 10:12 He hath made the world by his power, he hath established the world by his wisdom, and hath stretched out the heavens by his discretion.

Acts 17:24–25 God that made the world all things therein, seeing that he is Lord of heaven and earth, dwelleth not in temples made with hands. Neither is he worshipped with men's hands, as though he needs anything, seeing he giveth to all life, and breath, and all things.

Romans 1:20 For the invisible things of him from the creation of the world are clearly seen, being understood by the things that are made even his eternal power and Godhead.

Romans 11:36 Of Him, and through Him and to Him, are all things, to whom be glory forever... .

1 Corinthians 8:6 To us there is but one God, the father, of whom are all things, and we in Him, and one Lord Jesus Christ, by whom are all things, and we by him.

Hebrews 11:3 By faith we understand that the worlds were framed by the word of God, so that things which are seen were not made of things which do appear.

Humans have expressed an understanding of the existence of an all-powerful God throughout history. Our ability to understand God's creation is limited, as evidenced by the passing of thousands of years before some of the most simple and basic laws of nature were discovered and understood. For instance, it wasn't until the seventeenth century that the scientist Sir Isaac Newton was able to grasp and explain the physical law of gravity. People in the 21st century often think that this law has always been understood. In addition to the known "laws" of nature, God's power is accompanied by other supernatural attributes. We can see and understand this truth, but it is only by faith do we understand.

God's Power and Man's Will

Human beings are unquestionably the most superior beings on earth. Our intelligence, emotions, reasoning process, creative capacity, and survival ability in a range of environments and circumstances distinguish us from all other creatures. It would seem, based on the superior nature of the human being, that there would be no limits on our freedom and independence. The Bible refutes this idea. God's will has always been greater than the human will. Consider the Bible account of (1) the universal flood and destruction of wicked people in Noah's day (Genesis 6–8); (2) the defeat of rebellious people who tried to build a tower to reach heaven (Genesis 11); (3) the repeated punishment and ultimate destruction of the Jews and Israel (2 Kings); (4) the destruction of first century Jerusalem (Matthew 24); and (5) the prediction of Daniel about world powers and their collapse (Daniel 2). God is and always has been in control of everything.

God's Power over Life and Death

Humans cannot create life and cannot prevent death. Scientists have been able to manipulate the components necessary to reproduce living creatures and produce "test tube" babies, but they cannot create the components for life. They cannot create the eggs and sperm necessary for the formation of a new creature of a given species. They cannot create life from the dust of the earth. Billions of dollars are spent every year to extend life, but nothing can be done to destroy death as the ultimate fate of every living thing. Life and death are subject only to God's power. Consider the Bible's explanation of these:

Acts 17:28 For in Him we live and move and have our being... .

Genesis 2:7 The LORD God formed man of the dust of the ground and breathed into his nostrils the breath of life, and man became a living being.

Deuteronomy 8:3 Man does not live by bread only, but by every word that proceedeth out of the mouth of the LORD.

Job 27:3 All the while my breath is in me, and the spirit of God is in my nostrils.

Psalms 68:20 Unto God the LORD belong the issues from death.

Ecclesiastes 12:7 Then shall the dust return to the earth as it was; and the spirit shall return unto God who gave it.

Acts 17:25 He giveth to all life, and breath and all things ... .

1 Timothy 6:13 I urge you in the sight of God who gives life to all things ... .

2 Samuel 14:14 For we will surely die and become like water spilled on the ground, which cannot be gathered up again.

Job 30:23 For I know that thou will bring me to death, and to the house appointed for all living.

Psalms 49:7–10 None of them can by any means redeem his brother, nor give to God a ransom for him, that he should still live forever and not see corruption. For he seeth that wise men die, likewise the fool, and the brutish person perish.

Ecclesiastes 3:2 A time to be born, and a time to die ... .

Hebrews 9:27 And it is appointed unto men once to die, but after this the judgment.

Power over life and death is confined to God's realm of control. Humans must simply accept the fact that we cannot conquer death, and we can live due only to God's will and power. It is only through God that we can attain eternal life through our trust and surrender to God and his power over death.

The Human Response to God's Power

God's love for humans is greater than any power on earth. God was willing to offer his Son (John 3:16) to save humans from the destructive power of sin and death. As humans, we do not have the power to save ourselves from death and create our own eternal destiny (Acts 4:12). God has given the conditions of eternal life for humans (Acts 2:36–38). The powers over life, death, and eternal life are controlled by God and God only. Consider the words in 1 Corinthians 15:50–58:

> Now this I say, brethren, that flesh and blood cannot inherit the kingdom of God; nor does corruption inherit incorruption. Behold I tell you a mystery: We shall not all sleep, but we shall all be changed in a moment, in the twinkling of an eye, at the last trumpet. For the trumpet will sound, and the dead will be raised incorruptible, and we shall be changed. For this corruptible must put on incorruption, and this mortal must put on immortality. So when this corruption has put on incorruption, and this mortal has put on immortality, then shall be brought to pass the saying that is written: 'Death is swallowed up in victory. O death, where is your sting, O Hades, where is your victory?' The sting of death is sin, and the strength of sin is the law. But thanks be to God, who gives us the victory though our Lord Jesus Christ. Therefore, my beloved brethren, be steadfast, immovable, always abounding in the work of the Lord, knowing that your labor is not in vain in the Lord.

God's Supreme Being and place of sovereign control over every person and all creation must be accepted and respected. This should not arouse fear or concern for us, but rather it should be of comfort to us to know that God is in control. For, indeed, God promises to consider our every need (Matthew 6; Romans 8). He created us and intends us to spend eternity with Him in an eternal home, namely heaven. However, not everyone accepts God's sovereignty, which forces them to live in another eternal condition away from God, usually called Hell in the Bible. In light of these things, God's power is needed to save us from death, not just physical death but spiritual death, just as it was used to resurrect His Son from the dead (John 5:21; John 11:23).

God is all powerful. He is in control of all things. He has the power to end the existence of everything we know about (2 Peter 3:10-13). Our eternal destiny is within the control and power of God. We are powerless to prevent or avoid our own deaths, but God has offered us a way to live eternally with Him in heaven (John 14:1-6; Romans 1:16). We must acknowledge His great love and power to please Him.

Questions for Thought and Discussion

1. How does the term El Shaddai illustrate God's almighty power?
2. What accomplishments of God can never be replicated by humans?

3. Does man's free will have a limit imposed by
    God? What is that limit?
4. How is God's almighty power reflected in 1
    Corinthians 15:50–58?
5. Should the fact that God has ultimate control
    over us be a matter of fear or of comfort? Why?

I AM Omniscient

Joseph A. Barrier

"Great is our Lord, and mighy in power; His understanding is beyond measure" (Psalm 147:5). When reading this verse, it is clear that we are speaking of a God who knows and understands much more than we can comprehend. In this chapter, we will explore the omniscience (the ability to know all things) of God by looking at the information from the Bible.

God has revealed Himself to us in two ways. The first revelation is creation:

> ... because what may be known of God is manifest in them, for God has shown it to them. For since the creation of the world His invisible attributes are clearly seen, being understood by the things that are made, even His eternal power and Godhead ... (Romans 1:19–20).

The second way He reveals Himself to us is through His word, the Bible.

The secret things belong to the LORD our God, but those things which are revealed belong to us and to our children forever, that we may do all the words of this law" (Deuteronomy 29:29).

This verse also tells us the reason why God has revealed Himself to us through the Bible—so that we may obey Him. These are the only two avenues through which we come to know about God, and through both of them, we can go only as far as the scriptures take us. It is by using scripture that we can understand, to some degree, God whose wisdom is "beyond our understanding." It must also be stated that it is nearly impossible to speak of one quality of God without speaking of another. It is hard to speak of God's love without speaking of His mercy, or of His justice without speaking of His goodness. Therefore, some of the verses used in this chapter may be used in other chapters to describe other qualities of God.

God Knows You

O LORD, You have searched me and known me. You know my sitting down and my rising up; You understand my thought afar off. You comprehend my path and my lying down, and are acquainted with all my ways. Even before a word is on my tongue, O LORD, You know it completely (Psalm 139: 1–4).

God knows you. He knows all about you. He knows what you look like, where you come from, where you are going, and where you have been. He knows what you are thinking. He knows what you will think, say, and do. He knows everything about you. The Lord has searched us, and He knows us. It is good that He knows us.

> Are not two sparrows sold for a copper coin? And not one of them falls to the ground apart from your Father's will. But the very hairs of your head are all numbered. Do not fear therefore; you are of more value than many sparrows (Matthew 10:29–31).

This means that God knows when even the smallest and seemingly insignificant creatures die. We are so much more important to Him. He knows all about you because He cares about you.

God Sees Everything

"And there is no creature hidden from His sight, but all things are naked and open to the eyes of Him to whom we must give account" (Hebrews 4:13). God sees everything. No creature, no man, no beast, no fish, no amoeba, no bird ... nothing can hide from God. You cannot go into your house, into a closet, and under the covers to leave the presence of God. You cannot go into a forest under shade of trees and leave the presence of God. No one and nothing can hide from God. Our most secret things are exposed. We are as if we were open, with our hands outstretched and naked. Nothing to hide. Nothing can be hidden behind our backs. God can see it all. Proverbs 15:3 says, "The eyes of the Lord are in every place, keeping watch on the evil and the good." Psalm 139:7–10 tells us more:

> Where can I go from Your Spirit? Or where can I flee from Your presence? If I ascend into heaven, You are there; If I make my bed in hell, behold, You are there. If I take the wings of the morning, and dwell in the uttermost parts of the sea, even there Your hand shall lead me, and Your right hand shall hold me.

God sees all that happens in the world, good or evil. We cannot escape and go out to do evil at night because we believe God will not be there ... He will be there. He is there now, watching, helping when asked, hoping that those in sin will accept Him and His son Jesus. His eyes are also on the good. He is watching and helping His followers. We know that God will always be with us. Jesus promised that He would be with those who follow Him forever (Matthew 28:18–20). He sees the good and the bad.

"The LORD looks from heaven; He sees all the sons of men" (Psalm 33:13). In this verse, we have a picture of God in heaven, as if He is looking down. I once went to a tall mountain that had a tower on top of it. From the base of the mountain, I could not see far. I could only see trees around me, but could not see past them. I climbed the mountain and the tower to the top. I could see for miles and miles. I could see a river flowing miles away. I saw fields, villages, cities, and even more mountains in the distance. But even then, I could not see over the mountains. There was a limit to what I could see. God in heaven has the clearest view. He can see everything, even over the tallest mountains, over every obstacle. God has the best view. Not only does He see us, He understands us.

> The LORD looks from heaven; He sees all the sons of men. From the place of His dwelling He looks on all the inhabitants of the earth; He fashions their hearts individually; He considers (understands) all their works (Psalm 33:13–15).

God Understands Everything

"Great is our Lord, and mighty in power; His understanding is infinite (beyond measure)" (Psalm 147:5). God understands everything. He understands more than we can measure, and His understanding is beyond our comprehension. Many times I have to go to a quiet room in order to think deeply. If I have any distractions, I cannot concentrate. God, on the other hand, never has to stop and think deeply in order to understand a problem or situation. He already knows the problem and the solution. "The LORD by wisdom founded the earth; by understanding He established the heavens; by His knowledge the depths were broken up, and clouds drop down the dew" (Proverbs 3:19–20). How many humans could know how to create the earth with all of its complexities? We are learning new things everyday. It is impossible to know all about the earth, but God has always known. He made it. We have also studied the human body for thousands of years, and every day we make new discoveries. God has always understood how the body works, functions, and lives. God created the body. God gave us life. We, on the other hand, are not capable of creating life in these same ways. Scientists have tried for years to create life, but cannot do it. We do not understand how. God alone completely understands the processes of creation. We have also studied the stars and the planets ever since the world was created, and learned that it is very complex. Gravitational forces, the moon and the tides, the perfection of the distance of the earth to the sun, the atmosphere ... God in His wisdom created and placed all that we know where it is today by His understanding. We still have many questions about His creation, but He has none. God already knows. He understands everything.

In Job 38–41, God asks a series of questions concerning Job's understanding of the things that God has created. "Where were you when I laid the foundations of the earth? Tell Me, if you have understanding." "Did you set the measurements of the earth?" "Did you decide what the measurements of the sea would be?" Did man decide how high sea level would be? "Have you ever caused the sun to rise and set?" No human can do this. No human understands how this began. "Did you decide how long the day would be?" Why does each day have 24 hours? By the end of every day we are tired and ready for bed. What if the day was 40 hours long? We would not be able to stay awake all day long. We would also wake up in the middle of the night because no one sleeps 20 hours straight. The day is just long enough to give the plants sufficient sunlight without scorching them. The night is just long enough to let the plants recover without causing them to die from lack of sunlight. Did a human decide how this would be done? No human could do this.

Even if a human had decided it, he would not have been able to create it. "Did you decide that water would evaporate, forming clouds, and then rain upon the land?" This is a very complicated way to get water back to the land. God did this, not humans. "Did you cause the water to form ice when it reaches a specific temperature?" He continues to ask more and more questions, each causing us to realize that God knows everything. He understands so much more than we can comprehend. We know so little while God understands everything.

God Knows the Future

> Daniel answered and said: "Blessed be the name of God forever and ever, for wisdom and might are His. And He changes the times and the seasons; He removes kings and raises up kings; He gives wisdom to the wise and knowledge to those who have understanding. He reveals deep and secret things; He knows what is in the darkness, and light dwells with Him" (Daniel 2:20–22).

This understanding causes us to ask how He knows so much. Can He see into the future? How can these world events be under His control? God tells us in the book of Isaiah 46:8–10:

> Remember this, and show yourselves men; recall to mind, O you transgressors. Remember the former things of old, for I am God, and there is no other; I am God, and there is none like Me, declaring the end from the

beginning, and from ancient times things that are not yet done, saying, "My counsel shall stand, And I will do all My pleasure."

The Lord God wants all people to understand and remember that He alone is God. There is no one else like Him. He is unique. He tells us the beginning and the end. This is what is unique about God. Who else can tell us the beginning and the end? Only God was at the beginning. We know about it because He has told us about it. We don't remember our own births, but we still know the details—we know what day we were born, whether it was in a hospital, the time we were born, even our weight. How do we know these things? We know them because our parents or someone else who was there told us. Usually this information is written down in record form. In the case of the creation of the universe, "In the beginning God created the heavens and the earth" (Genesis 1:1). God told us that He was there. Only God can say this, and only God can tell us what will happen in the end.

God has a purpose, and He will accomplish it. How does He know it will be accomplished? Psalm 139:4 says, "Even before a word is on my tongue, O Lord, You know it completely." Before we speak, God knows what we will say.

For You formed my inward parts; You covered me in my mother's womb. I will praise You, for I am fearfully and wonderfully made; marvelous are Your works, and that my soul knows very well. My frame was not hidden from You, when I was made in secret, and skillfully wrought in the lowest parts of the earth. Your eyes saw my substance, being yet unformed. And in Your book they all were written, the days fashioned for me, when as yet there were none of them (Psalm 139:13–16).

This psalm speaks of a book—a biography of yourself—with God being the author. The special thing about this book is that it has already been written. It was written before you were born and before you were even formed—when you were just a mass of cells in your mother's womb. God knows your future, and He knows His future. God has a plan.

The last book of the New Testament contains prophesies of the end times. It tells of a time when all who have lived and died on this earth will be judged. Those who do not obey the Lord will be cast into the lake of fire, but all those who have believed and obeyed will inherit everlasting life with God in heaven. How do we know that this will come to pass? How does God know? We know because God, who knows all, sees all, and understands all, has said it will happen. He is eternal; therefore He knows past, present, and future. Isaiah 57:15 says,

> For thus says the High and Lofty One who inhabits eternity, whose name is Holy: "I dwell in the high and holy place, with him who has a contrite and humble spirit, to revive the spirit of the humble, and to revive the heart of the contrite ones."

This tells us that God dwells, or lives, outside of time, in eternity. Time is part of His creation. He dwells in heaven. He sees all. He has the best view—only now we understand that He not only sees the world as it is before us, but sees the past, present, and future all at once. Psalm 90:2 says, "Before the mountains were brought forth, or ever You had formed the earth and the world, even from everlasting to everlasting, You are God." Psalm 90:4 also says, "For a thousand years in Your sight are like yesterday when it is past, and like a watch in the night." This is hard to comprehend, but we must remember that God's understanding is beyond measure. We must understand that God knows the future. God knows all.

God Knows All

"Every good gift and every perfect gift is from above, and comes down from the Father of lights, with whom there is no variation or shadow of turning" (James 1:17). Because God knows all, He does not change. No variation at all. Not even a shadow, a hint, a minute change—no change at all. That is, the nature or character of God remains the same, no matter what.

On the other hand, many scriptures speak of God changing His mind in reaction to man's obedience or disobedience. In Exodus 32, for example, God became angry with the people of Israel because they had forsaken Him by building an idol and worshiping it. God was so angry that He promised to destroy the rebellious people of Israel. He was reacting against their sin.

However, Moses pled with God, begging Him not to destroy them. Exodus 32:14 says, "So the Lord relented from the harm which He said He would do to His people." The Lord relented, changed, or repented. He changed His mind. He did not destroy the people. He again reacted to human choice, this time to the prayer that Moses offered.

God's nature does not change, but His response to us does change, due to our faith or lack of faith, which He foresees. Obviously God does not receive new information, because He knows all. Present, past, future, our hearts, our minds—everything is known by God. God cannot receive new information because there is nothing that He does not already know. In addition God cannot have a change of heart, because a change for the better would mean that He is not already perfect. Habakkuk 1:13 says, "You are of purer eyes than to behold evil, and cannot look on wickedness." A change for the worse would mean that God would become imperfect. This verse has just said that God cannot sin; therefore God cannot change to become imperfect.

In God's infinite knowledge, because He sees the end from the beginning, He must know in advance—before we ever obey or disobey—what free choices we will make. When we make those choices, whether good or bad, God responds as He always knew He would, in keeping with His perfect, unchanging character. God's omniscience does not minimize the importance of each decision we make. If we disobey God, He will respond in judgment. If we repent and obey, He will then respond instead in gracious forgiveness.

God, knowing all things, knew that the Israelites would disobey Him. When they did, He responded and threatened to destroy them. God also knew that Moses would plead with Him to spare their lives. So, when Moses prayed, God responded to him and relented. Remember, their biographies were already known by God. God knew how everything would happen then, and He knows what will happen today tomorrow and until the end of time. "God is not a man, that He should lie, nor a son of man, that He should repent. Has He said, and will He not do? Or has He spoken, and will He not make it good?" (Numbers 23:19). And again, "For I am the LORD, I do not change; therefore you are not consumed, O sons of Jacob" (Malachi 3:6).

Conclusion

By studying the Bible, you can have a better understanding of the one, true, all knowing God who sees and understands you, and who knows what the future holds for you. I hope this chapter has helped you understand just a small part of God and what He knows. I hope that you understand that God is aware of you. "For the ways of man are before the eyes of the LORD, and He ponders all his paths" (Proverbs 5:21). He doesn't watch over you because He is a spy or a busybody, but because He cares for you.

> Are not two sparrows sold for a copper coin? And not one of them falls to the ground apart from your Father's will. But the very hairs of your head are all numbered. Do not fear therefore; you are of more value than many sparrows (Matthew 10:29–31).

He cares for you more than birds or any living creature.

Where can I go from Your Spirit? Or where can I flee from Your presence? If I ascend into heaven, You are there; if I make my bed in hell, behold, You are there. If I take the wings of the morning, and dwell in the uttermost parts of the sea, even there Your hand shall lead me, and Your right hand shall hold me (Psalm 139:7–10).

The purpose of His knowing us is to lead us as a friend would lead another friend who is blind or cannot see the way. We must follow the all-knowing God by listening and obeying His direction as provided through His words. Remember, we cannot fool God. He cannot be tricked. He knows if we are truly seeking Him. He knows if we are truly following as He leads, for *God knows everything*.

Questions for Thought and Discussion

1. In what ways has God revealed Himself to us? Why might He have chosen these specific ways?
2. How does Psalm 139 illustrate the omniscience of God? How many specific manifestations of His omniscience are mentioned in the chapter?
3. How does God's knowledge of the future affect our lives today?
4. What is God's concept of time? How does it differ from ours?
5. Why does God choose to know every detail of our lives?

I AM Omnipresent

Bill Bagents

The Bible teaches that God stands outside the limitations of time and space. In that "God is Spirit" (John 4:24), He is not bound by laws of physics. Nowhere is this taught more clearly than in Psalm 139. Linking the concepts of God's omniscience (all-knowing) and omnipotence (all-powerful), Psalm 139 begins by asserting that God understands our thoughts before we complete them, He comprehends our motives before we translate them into action, and He even knows our words before we speak them. In the words of Jeremiah 20:12, God can "see the mind and heart."

Concerning God's omnipresence (present everywhere), Psalm 139:7 asks, "Where can I go from Your Spirit? Or where can I flee from Your presence?" It is not that the psalmist wants to flee God's presence. Rather, he is celebrating the fact that God will always be with him no matter where he goes. From the highest heaven to the underworld, the psalmist says to God, "You are there!"

David, one of the writers of the Psalms, anticipates such presence in Psalm 23:4, "Yea, though I walk through the valley of the shadow of death, I will fear no evil: for You are with me; Your rod and Your staff, they comfort me." If wings could fly the psalmist to the uttermost parts of the sea, God is there. Darkness or light, God is present. The Bible presents God as eyewitness to every action in every place at all times. Nothing is hidden from His sight.

The doctrine of God's omnipresence is taught in many places in the Bible. Jeremiah 23:23–24 reads, "'Am I a God near at hand,' says the LORD, 'and not a God afar off? Can anyone hide himself in secret places so I shall not see him?' says the LORD; 'Do I not fill heaven and earth?" says the LORD." God first spoke these words to false prophets who claimed to speak in His name. He used these questions to document the futility of their actions. How can one think that his words will go unnoticed if the God of heaven is everywhere at all times? From the perspective of the righteous, 1 Peter 3:12 quotes Psalm 34:15, "For the eyes of the LORD are on the righteous, and His ears are open to their prayers ..." The Bible presents God as one who will neither leave nor forsake His people (Hebrews 13:5).

In addition to such direct statements, the Bible also dramatically asserts God's omnipresence through many strong, but less direct statements. Concerning our words, Matthew 12:36 records the teaching of Jesus, "But I say to you that for every idle word men may speak, they will give account of it in the day of judgment." That statement assumes God's omnipresence. How else could God know every word that humans speak? Consider Hagar and Ishmael as they are sent away from Abraham's camp.

When they fell into distress in the wilderness, " … God heard the voice of the lad" (Genesis 21:17). God heard because He was present to hear!

When Jesus asks, "Are not five sparrows sold for two copper coins? And not one of them is forgotten by God," He implies the omnipresence of God (Luke 12:6). When Jesus says, "But the very hairs of your head are all numbered," He implies both God's omniscience and His omnipresence (Luke 12:7). More than that, He reminds us of God's ongoing personal concern for His creation.

When Jesus speaks of doing charitable deeds, praying, and fasting secretly so as to bring glory to God, He uses very similar phrases in describing God's blessings:

> Matthew 6:4 … And your Father who sees in secret will Himself reward you openly.

> Matthew 6:6 … And your Father who sees in secret will reward you openly.

> Matthew 6:18 … Do not appear to men to be fasting, but to your Father who is in the secret place; and He will reward you openly.

God not only sees in the secret place, He is *in the secret place*. Because of His omnipresence, He is eyewitness to every good deed that we do.

When Jesus (the son of God) promises, "For where two or three are gathered together in My name, I am there in the midst of them" (Matthew 18:20), He is not speaking poetically. Rather, He is speaking prophetically. When

Jesus ascended from earth to return to the Father in heaven (Acts 1), He resumed all the attributes of deity shared with His Father, which He had before coming to earth to live as a human in a body limited in time and space. He resumed omnipresence, allowing Him to be with His people in all places at all times. Thus, His promise at the time of His ascension back to His Father, " ... And lo, I am with you always, even to the end of the age" (Matthew 28:20).

Concerning the great and final day of judgment, the apostle Paul writes, "For we must all appear before the judgment seat of Christ, that each one may receive the things done in the body, according to what he has done, whether good or bad" (2 Corinthians 5:10). The passage assumes that God knows all that has been done, thereby implying His omnipresence. The point is even stronger in Luke 8:17. Jesus says, "For nothing is secret that will not be revealed, nor anything hidden that will not be known and come to light." God knows our conduct because He is ever present to observe it.

Apparent Contradictions

Students of the Bible have asked, "If God is present every-where at all times, then why does the Bible speak of God's coming and going, His arrival and departure?" Genesis 3 records an important, tragic interaction between Eve and the serpent. As part of that interaction, both Eve and Adam sin. Guilt and fear enter their hearts for the first time. Where is God when this is happening? More than that, Genesis 3:8 mentions Adam and Eve hearing "the sound of the LORD God walking in the garden in the cool of the day, and Adam and his wife hid themselves from the presence of the LORD God among the trees of the garden."

Sometimes, questions are best answered by questions. Does the fact that the presence of God is not mentioned earlier in Genesis 3 mean that He was absent? Does the fact that God allowed Adam and Eve to perceive the sound of His movement in the garden mean that God was incapable of silent movement? Does the fact that Adam and Eve attempted to hide from God's presence mean that such is possible? Though the LORD spoke to them, asking, "Where are you?" could He not have done so to give them opportunity to respond and begin a conversation?

Many times the Bible speaks of God appearing to people. Some have asserted that this language implies that God is not omnipresent. For example, Genesis 17:1 records God's appearance to Abram to reaffirm His covenant. Genesis 18:1 records that the LORD appeared to Abraham using the form of three men. The biblical teaching of God's omnipresence does not assert that God is always visible to the human eye. Quite the contrary, even within the Bible direct visible manifestations of God's presence are rare. Such manifestations are reserved for occasions of special commission, encouragement, or communication. Reports of God's visible, dramatic presence do not deny the doctrine of His omnipresence throughout the world.

In Psalm 51:11, a heartbroken and penitent David pleads with God in these words, "Do not cast me away from Your presence, and do not take your Holy Spirit from me." Thus the question, "If God is omnipresent, how could David fear that God would cast him away from His presence? How can a person be cast from the presence of an omnipresent being?"

The Bible recognizes different levels or types of God's presence. From a general perspective, God is everywhere and all is within His presence. From a relational perspective, only those who walk with God on His terms are deemed worthy to live in His presence. Recognizing this truth, Psalm 15:1 asks, "LORD, who may dwell in Your tabernacle? Who may dwell in Your holy hill?" A series of moral and ethical answers follows. Only the person who walks in righteousness, speaks truth, opposes evil, and keeps his word can live with God. Psalm 24:3 asks virtually the same question and gives a shorter version of the same answer. The full blessings of God's presence are reserved for those whose lives honor Him.

Several Challenges to Omnipresence

Thoughtful students have asked, "If God is omnipresent, then tell me how evil exists? How do so many terrible things happen if God is everywhere?" Students of the Bible do not deny the presence and power of evil in this world. For example, Cain killed his brother, Abel (Genesis 4). God saw this conflict coming. He intervened, asking Cain three excellent questions:

- Why are you angry?
- And why has your countenance fallen?
- If you do well, will you not be accepted?

God said to Cain, "And if you do not do well, sin lies at the door. And its desire is for you, but you should rule over it" (Genesis 4:7). God did not remove Cain's ability to choose his actions. God allowed Cain to control his own behavior. God's presence and intervention did not prevent the murder of Abel.

Similarly, as Stephen was being opposed by a religious mob, he saw "the heavens opened and the Son of Man standing at the right hand of God" (Acts 7:56). Rather than leading to Stephen's protection or the repentance of the mob, Stephen's description of what he saw infuriated them to the point of murder. Even direct perception of the presence of God did not change the physical reality of Stephen's situation. In a world where God allows people to choose their actions, God's presence does not overrule their behavior.

Classic Misunderstandings of God's Omnipresence

Some affirm God's omnipresence from a non-biblical perspective. Some have reasoned, "Certainly, God is present everywhere and at all times. This is obvious because all that we see is God. There is no distinction between Creator and creation. All is one in seamless unity." Others take a more moderate position, affirming, "Certainly, God is present everywhere and at all times. This has to be true because there is something of God in everything that God has made." These statements do not agree with the biblical teaching of the omnipresence of God.

Clearly, the Bible teaches that God created all that

exists. The Bible begins with these words, "In the beginning God created the heavens and the earth" (Genesis 1:1). Psalm 19:1 adds, "The heavens declare the glory of God, and the firmament shows His handiwork." Colossians 1:15–17 says of Jesus Christ,

> He is the image of the invisible God, the firstborn over all creation. For by Him all things were created that are in heaven and that are on earth, visible and invisible, whether thrones or dominions or principalities or powers. All things were created through Him and for Him. He is before all things, and in Him all things consist.

Hebrews 1:2 speaks of Jesus Christ as God's " ... Son, whom He has appointed heir of all things; through whom He made the worlds."

While God made the worlds and loves His creation, the Bible recognizes a strong and consistent distinction between the Creator and His creation. The Bible never asserts that every aspect of creation is somehow divine, containing something that is God. Of all creation, only humanity is said to be created in the image of God (Genesis 1:26–27). Even affirming that fact, the Bible still recognizes a dramatic difference between the Creator and His creation. Psalm 95:6–7 affirms, "O come, let us worship and bow down; let us kneel before the LORD our Maker, for He is our God, and we are the people of His pasture, and the sheep of His hand." Though He honored us by making us in His image, "a little lower than the angels, and You have crowned him with glory and honor" (Psalm 8:5), we are very weak in comparison to God (See Jeremiah 10:23 and Job 37–41). As taught in Isaiah 55:8–9, "'For My thoughts are not your thoughts, nor are your ways My ways,' says the LORD. 'For as the heavens are higher than the earth, so are My ways higher than your ways, and My thoughts than your thoughts.'"

While God made the worlds and loves His creation, God tells us that His creation is not pennanent. God intends to take the faithful home to heaven. Of this earth, 2 Peter 3: 10 says,

> But the day of the Lord will come as a thief in the night, in which the heavens will pass away with a great noise, and the elements will melt with fervent heat; both the earth and the works that are in it will be burned up.

The physical universe will be destroyed, but the spiritual universe endures forever.

From a Christian perspective, some have proposed that the omnipresence of God guarantees that nothing truly evil or damaging will ever happen to a faithful believer. They assert that passages including Romans 8:31–39 and Ephesians 3:20–21 guarantee God's ongoing protection from all types of harm. Sadly, they fail to see that Romans 8:35 acknowledges that Christians can face tribulation, distress, persecution, famine, nakedness, peril and sword. They fail to remember that Paul was in prison when he wrote the letter to the Ephesians. They fail to remember the many negative challenges that Paul endured for the sake of the gospel (2 Corinthians 11:22–28). They fail to remember the direct statements of 1 Peter 2:19–20, that one can "'endure grief, suffering wrongly" and one can "do good and suffer." While we greatly appreciate the fact that God stands with His people in all their trials, God's omnipresence does not shield Christians from all trials.

What Difference Does The Omnipresence of God Make to Me?

Some view the omnipresence of God negatively. They think of the concept as being spied upon and having their privacy violated. The Bible never presents the omnipresence of God in such terms. In fact, the Bible warns against the danger of forgetting the omniscience and omnipresence of God. Psalm 10:8–13 describes an evil person who lurks in secret places as he plots theft and murder. Verse 11 details the flawed thinking that leads the evil person to such actions: "He has said in his heart, 'God has forgotten; He hides His face; He will never see.'" Psalm 94:4–7 echoes this thought. The wicked speak insolently, afflict God's people, and even resort to murder, saying, "The Lord does not see, nor does the God of Jacob understand." This error is so grave that the next verse labels those who espouse it "senseless among the people" and "fools" (Psalm 94:8). What a dangerous state in which to live!

Christians welcome the omnipresence of God as an act of homage and submission. The psalm that speaks most directly to God's omnipresence ends with these words, "Search me, O God, and know my heart. Try me and know my anxieties. See if there is any wicked way in me, and lead me in the way everlasting." The psalmist welcomes God's presence and God's complete knowledge of his heart and life. He trusts God with his life and his soul. As Acts 17:28 acknowledges, " ... For in Him we live and move and have our being, as also some of our own poets have said, 'For we are also His offspring.'" In the words of Psalm 100:3, "Know that the LORD, He is God. It is He who has made us and not we ourselves. We are His people and the sheep of His pasture." Because God is creator and sustainer, He has every right to be present in our lives. Because God is gracious and loving, we want Him to be present with us every moment. Christians view the omnipresence of God as one of His greatest blessings, a tremendous manifestation of grace. Belief in the omnipresence of God provides many benefits to God's people.

God's presence acts as a deterrent to sin. If God is everywhere and knows all, there is no provision for hiding sin. " ... Be sure your sin will find you out" stands as a barrier to willful, rebellious sin (Numbers 32:23b). Loyalty to God, the fact that He hates sin, and the knowledge that He sees all strongly encourage righteousness. We see this in the life of Joseph. When tempted by Potiphar's wife, Joseph's refusal was accompanied by these words, "How then can I do this great wickedness and sin against God?" (Genesis 39:9)

God's presence ensures that no good deed will go unnoticed. As noted above, this is clearly taught in Matthew 6:1, 4, 6, and 18. Matthew 10:40–42 records a promise of reward stated by Jesus. It ends by saying, '"And whoever gives one of these little ones only a cup of cold water in the name of a disciple, assuredly, I say to you he shall by no means lose his reward." God's omnipresence guarantees that every good work is known and appreciated by God. In Matthew 25:34–40, Jesus declares that He takes such works personally: "Assuredly I say to you, inasmuch as you did it to one of the least of these My brethren, you did it to Me."

God's omnipresence ensures that the Christian is never alone as he or she endures temptation or stress. Hebrews 13:5 uses God's words of Deuteronomy 31:6 and 8, "I will never leave you nor forsake you." Hebrews 13:6 reads, "So we may boldly say, 'The LORD is my helper; I will not fear; What can man do to me?'" Paul echoes this concept in Philippians 4:13, "I can do all things through Christ who strengthens me." In the context of Philippians 4, "do" means "endure" or "overcome."

God's omnipresence offers spiritual and emotional comfort to the believer. In the language of the shepherd, David says, "Yea, though I walk through the valley of the shadow of death, I will fear no evil; for You are with me; Your rod and Your staff, they comfort me" (Psalm 23:4). In Psalm 145:17–20, David adds,

> The LORD is righteous in all His ways, gracious in all His works. The LORD is near to all who call upon Him, to all who call upon Him in truth. He will fulfill the desire of those who fear Him; He also will hear their cry and save them. The LORD preserves all who love Him...

Many biblical examples prove that God's preservation of those who love Him may be spiritual salvation rather than protection here on earth. No matter the level of protection, the comfort of God's presence is real.

God's omnipresence means that God is always available

to hear our prayers. This gift is not to be accepted presumptuously. Rather, it is a precious blessing. 1 Peter 3:12 quotes Psalm 34:15–16, "For the eyes of the LORD are on the righteous, and His ears are open to their prayers; but the face of the LORD is against those who do evil." The privilege of being heard favorably by God is directly linked both to our conduct and our faith (1 Peter 3:8–12; James 1:5–8). God's ability to hear the prayers of all the faithful is compelling evidence of His power and majesty. God's willingness to be present with His children and to care for us is compelling evidence of His goodness and His grace.

Conclusion

The Bible clearly teaches that God is omnipresent (Psalm 139:7–12). This truth is taught through numerous proofs, both direct and indirect. The willingness of God to be near to us demonstrates His love and concern. The blessings of His presence are greater than our ability to state or comprehend. God's omnipresence calls on us to live consistently in the light of His love and truth. It offers us a foretaste of life in heaven where we will see Him face to face forever.

Questions for Thought and Discussion

1. How does Matthew 6 teach the concept of God's omnipresence?
2. How can God be in every place at every time?

3. What is the difference between God's presence in a general sense and His presence in the life of a Christian?
4. Does God's omnipresence prevent bad things from happening? Why or why not?
5. Why is God's omnipresence a blessing as opposed to an intrusion?

I AM Merciful

Brad McKinnon

In his play, "The Merchant of Venice," William Shakespeare wrote that mercy "is enthroned in the hearts of kings, it is an attribute to God himself." By inspiration of God, the psalmist declared: "The Lord is merciful and gracious, slow to anger and abounding in steadfast love" (Psalm 103:8). As Moses acknowledged long ago, Yahweh is indeed "a merciful God" (Deuteronomy 4:31). The divine quality of mercy includes the ideas of care and trustworthiness, as Moses continued: " ... he will not abandon or destroy you or forget the covenant with your forefathers" (Deuteronomy 4:31). The God of the Bible is full of mercy, or, if you will, "merciful."

Generally, mercy can be defined as an act of favor or compassion. However, it also includes the concept of forbearance shown to an offender. So mercy is at the same time both an act of kindness and a choice not to act in vengeance. One might liken it to a parent who shows natural kindness to a child in providing for his or her needs, while at the same time showing compassion when the child, although doing his or her best, makes mistakes. In presenting the Ten Commandments to Moses at Mount Sinai, God described himself as "merciful and gracious, longsuffering, and abundant in goodness and truth" (Exodus 34:6). Thus, God's mercy is closely associated with grace (favor), longsuffering, goodness, truth, and even His commandments. Additionally, God's mercy highlights His sovereignty. To Moses, Yahweh said, "I will have mercy on whom I will have mercy, and I will have compassion on whom I will have compassion" (Exodus 33:19). The apostle Paul later quoted this passage, indicating that salvation in Christ is dependent on God's mercy: "'I will have mercy on whom I have mercy, and I will have compassion on whom I have compassion.' It does not, therefore, depend on man's desire or effort, but on God's mercy" (Romans 9:15).

Mercy has been described as the attribute of seeing life from the perspective of another individual and responding accordingly. God in His infinite wisdom and love is able to see things from our perspective and provide for our needs. The terms translated "merciful" or "mercy" occur 150 times in the Bible. The majority of these instances focus on God's mercy or His desire for us to show mercy to one another. The Bible underscores God's mercy by high-lighting the human need for mercy; by describing God's mercy in prophetic terms; by detailing the work of Jesus, the ultimate expression of God's mercy; by illustrating the significance of mercy through parables; and by emphasizing our own responsibility to be merciful.

The Human Need for Mercy

It is a universal characteristic of the human condition to need and desire mercy. At times we need mercy from others to help provide for our physical necessities, such as food, water, shelter, and clothing. We also have emotional needs like peace, comfort, and contentment. Above all, we have spiritual needs, including forgiveness, reconciliation, and fellowship. The fulfillment of these needs is ultimately a result of divine mercy. We as human beings have need of mercy from God in all its various manifestations. It is important to recognize that God created us in His image: "God created man in his own image, in the image of God he created him; male and female he created them" (Genesis 1:27). The psalmist declared, "Know that the Lord is God. It is he who made us, and we are his; we are his people, the sheep of his pasture" (Psalm 100:3). Therefore, God knows what we need, and we depend on Him completely for the fulfillment of those needs. This is true whether we acknowledge the source of these provisions or not. In fact, God knows what we need even before we ask Him. In a discussion about anxiety over the need for food and clothing, Jesus declared that our "heavenly Father knows that you need them" (Matthew 6:32). Thus, Jesus taught us to pray, "Give us today our daily bread" (Matthew 6:11) not for the purpose of providing God with information, but rather for our benefit. Interestingly, he also noted that God's physical blessings extend both to the good and the bad, for God "causes his sun to rise on the evil and the good, and sends rain on the righteous and the unrighteous" (Matthew 5:45).

Our most pressing need in regard to mercy is the forgiveness of sins and the resulting reconciliation with God. Paul declared, "all have sinned and fall short of the glory of God" (Romans 3:23). Thus, we all stand as those who have offended the holiness of God. Thankfully, however, just as sin is universal, God has a universal love and desire to bless with redemption those who obey him: "For God so loved the world that he gave his one and only Son, that whoever believes in him shall not perish but have eternal life" (John 3:16). With joy, we can celebrate the fact that God has provided a savior in Jesus Christ: "But because of his great love for us, God, who is rich in mercy, made us alive with Christ even when we were dead in transgressions—it is by grace you have been saved" (Ephesians 2:4–5). It is clear that the overriding emphasis, when it comes to God's mercy, is the forgiveness of sins that He offers through Jesus. In fact, the name "Jesus" means "Yahweh saves" or "Yahweh is salvation." As the angel of the Lord declared, before Jesus's birth: "he will save his people from their sins" (Matthew 1:21). Therefore, a detailed examination of God's mercy in the sense of forgiveness and reconciliation will be helpful to the one who desires to learn more about Yahweh and His will for our lives.

God's Mercy in Prophecy

One of the evidences for the Bible being from God is the abundance of fulfilled prophecies. There are literally thousands of prophecies in the Scriptures regarding individuals, nations, kingdoms, covenants, and the like that have been fulfilled in perfect detail One of the key components of many Old Testament prophecies is the promise of God's mercy in a special and complete way through Jesus Christ. None is more compelling than Jeremiah 31:31–34:

> "The time is coming," declares the Lord, "when I will make a new covenant with the house of Israel and with the house of Judah. It will not be like the covenant I made with their forefathers when I took them by the hand to lead them out of Egypt. . . This is the covenant I will make with the house of Israel after that time," declares the Lord. "I will put my law in their minds and write it on their hearts. I will be their God, and they will be my people ... For I will forgive their wickedness and will remember their sins no more."

Notice the passage states that the time was coming, when the Lord would make a new covenant, based on forgiveness of sin. In clear language, the Lord promises that He would no longer remember the sins of those in this covenant relationship. Many years later the Hebrews writer noted the fulfillment of this promise through Jesus Christ as "high priest, who sat down at the right hand of the throne of the Majesty in heaven" (Hebrews 8:1). To prove his point, the Hebrew writer quotes Jeremiah 31:31–34, reflecting on the concept of mercy or forgiveness (Hebrews 8:5–11).

Prophecy not only includes the prediction of future events, but it also has reference to the work of the man of God, acting as a herald or messenger for God. It is in this capacity that the psalmist in Psalm 136 praises God "for his mercy will have no end." The Old Testament book of Psalms is in essence an inspired Hebrew hymnbook. Included in this collection, Psalm 136, a song of praise to the Lord, concludes every verse with the phrase "his mercy endures forever." By examining each verse, one can find the reasons to praise God based on His mercy or love. First, one should give thanks to God because of who He is: "for he is good . . . the Lord of lords." Second, one should give thanks to God because of what He has done. The psalmist references the creation of the universe, God's deliverance of Israel from Egyptian slavery, and His providence in bringing them into the promised land (v. 4–24). Finally, he remembers God's care for all people (v. 25), declaring, "Give thanks to the God of heaven. His mercy endures forever" (v. 26). Likewise, we should praise God for simply being God and for all that He has done for us. Indeed, "his mercy endures forever."

Jesus: A Merciful High Priest

In Acts 10:38, the apostle Peter summarizes Jesus's ministry of mercy in this way: "he went around doing good and healing all who were under the power of the devil, because God was with him." Years before, regarding the promised birth of Jesus, His mother Mary declared that in giving His Son, Jesus, God was "remembering to be merciful to Abraham and his descendants forever, even as he said to our fathers" (Luke 1:54). This Jesus was one who showed compassion by using His power as God in the flesh to address the physical and emotional needs of the suffering, while ultimately providing for the universal spiritual needs of humanity by passively accepting suffering, for "when they hurled their insults at him, he did not retaliate; when he suffered, he made no threats" (1 Peter 2:23). Again, Jesus was the perfect embodiment of mercy—acting to alleviate suffering in others and refusing to act in personal retaliation in order to take care of our greatest need.

People that Jesus interacted with during His earthly ministry saw Him as one who could provide them mercy in the midst of desperate times and circumstances. In one instance, as Jesus traveled between Samaria and Galilee, ten lepers cried out to Him: "Jesus, Master, have mercy on us!" (Luke 17:13) They saw in Jesus one who could have compassion on them and heal them. They were not disappointed, because as they walked away they were cleansed. Unfortunately, only one of the ten returned to thank Jesus. It is important for us to remember to praise God for the mercy He extends to us, not just with words, but with a life of service to Him. Matthew records two separate instances when Jesus healed blind men at their request for mercy (Matthew 9:27; 20:30). Jesus was regularly moved with compassion for those who were suffering, healing them of their sicknesses (Matthew 14:14). Today these accounts help produce within us faith in Jesus, who can heal our spiritual sicknesses:

> Jesus did many other miraculous signs in the presence of his disciples, which are not recorded in this book. But these are written that you may believe that Jesus is the Christ, the Son of God, and that by believing you may have life in his name (John 20:30–31).

When one thinks of the spiritual manifestations of Jesus's mercy, they must be understood in terms of Jesus's role as the great high priest. An in-depth look at this idea from the book of Hebrews helps us understand the blessings that this kind of relationship brings to our lives. In Hebrews, the writer places emphasis on Jesus being the mediator of a better covenant than the covenant given through Moses. In so doing, he highlights Jesus's role as high priest. Hebrews 1:3 describes Jesus as performing the priestly function of the "purification of sins." In chapter 2, the writer notes that in order to provide an appeasing sacrifice to God on our behalf, Jesus had to share in our humanity: "For this reason he had to be made like his brothers in every way, in order that he might become a merciful and faithful high priest in service to God" (Hebrews 2:17). He continues by identifying Jesus as "the apostle and high priest whom we confess" (Hebrews 3:1).

In what sense can Jesus be our merciful and faithful high priest? First, he knows what it is like to suffer temptation. Because of this "he is able to help those who are being tempted" (Hebrews 2:18). However, as our perfect high priest, although tempted "in every way just as we are," He did so "without sin" (Hebrews 4:15). Thus, He is able to both "sympathize with our weaknesses" and provide mercy and grace "to help us in our time of need" (Hebrews 4:15–16). Jesus did not take this honor for Himself; rather He was designated by God as our high priest, becoming "the source of eternal salvation for all who obey him" (Hebrews 5:9–10). Therefore, Jesus has become priest in a better covenant, because He "lives forever . . . has a permanent priesthood" and "is able to save completely those who come to God through him" (Hebrews 7:24–25).

Jesus can and will meet our needs, which is the very definition of mercy, because He is "holy, blameless, pure, set apart from sinners, exalted above the heavens" (Hebrews 7:26), sacrificing Himself for our "sins once for all" (Hebrews 7:27). This sacrifice "has made perfect forever those who are being made holy" (Hebrews 10:14). What kind of response can we make, knowing that Jesus is "a great priest over the house of God?" (Hebrews 10:21) First, we can have confidence to enter the presence of God by Jesus's blood (Hebrews 10:19). Second, we can approach God's throne "with a sincere heart in full assurance of faith" (Hebrews 10:21). Third, we can "hold unswervingly to the hope we profess, for he who promised is faithful" (Hebrews 10:23). Fourth, we should "consider how we may spur one another on toward love and good deeds" (Hebrews 10:24). Again as Jesus declared: "Be merciful, just as your Father is merciful" (Luke 6:36).

The Parable of the Unmerciful Servant

Jesus often taught in parables. The word parable is a combination of two terms, one meaning "to throw" and the other meaning "beside." Therefore, a parable is a style of teaclting in which one takes a common earthly concept that is generally understood and places it beside a heavenly concept that may be more difficult to understand. The purpose of this form of teaching is to help the willing individual to have a better grasp of an important spiritual truth. When He was asked why He taught in parables,

Jesus responded by stating that the purpose was to reveal truth to those who were ready and willing to receive it, noting that "blessed are your eyes because they see, and your ears because they hear" (Matthew 13:16).

An important parable relating to God's mercy is Jesus's "Parable of the Unmerciful Servant," found in Matthew 18:23–35. The parable is the story of a servant who, after pleading for mercy, is forgiven a very large debt by his master. The servant's debt represents the debt of sin that God is willing to forgive. The story continues with the forgiven servant going out and demanding repayment of a very small debt owed to him by a fellow servant. This represents how we often treat one another. When the master finds out what the umnerciful servant has done, he orders him to be sent to the jailers until the debt is paid. Jesus concludes with this admonition: "This is how my heavenly Father will treat each of you unless you forgive your brother from your heart" (Matthew 18:35).

There are several important lessons that one should take away from this story. First, God is abundant in mercy. The servant in the parable was forgiven a debt of "ten thousand talents." This amount would have been an extremely large sum of money that the servant could never hope to repay. God, like the master in the story, is willing to forgive a debt that we could not possibly repay. Second, those who have received mercy have the responsibility of sharing the same with others. In the story, the forgiven, yet unforgiving, servant requires immediate repayment of an amount totaling "a hundred denarii," a very small amount compared to what he had owed. Third, if we are not merciful, then God will not extend mercy to us.

Be Merciful

Regarding our responsibility to be merciful, Jesus exhorted those who desired to be His disciples to "be merciful, just as your Father is merciful" (Luke 6:36). In presenting us with this seemingly impossible task, Jesus offers insight into the significance of being merciful as God is merciful. First, to be merciful like God means loving your enemies: "But I tell you who hear me: Love your enemies, do good to those who hate you, bless those who curse you, pray for those who mistreat you" (Luke 6:27–28). God loved us, when we were enemies of God because of our choice to sin. This kind of love is a choice that one makes; it is desiring what's best for the other individual. It is not necessarily based on tender emotions, but it is a love of the mind or will. Second, we are to give to others. God is a giver: "Every good and perfect gift is from above, coming down from the Father of the heavenly light, who does not change like shifting shadows" (James 1:17). God wants us to be givers so we can be more like him. If we give, Jesus has promised that "it will be given to you" (Luke 6:38). Third, to be merciful like God, we must obey what many have called the "Golden Rule": "Do to others as you would have them do to you" (Luke 6:31). Notice that Jesus did not merely say that we should avoid doing evil. It has been said that the Jewish Rabbi Hillel taught, "that which is despicable to you, do not do to your fellow." In contrast, Jesus demanded a higher standard, commanding us to act positively for the good of other people.

The apostle Paul offers praise to God, referring to our creator as "the Father of mercies" (2 Corinthians 1:3). The plural use of mercy is significant. It underscores the abundance of God's mercy, but it also emphasizes the fact that God's mercy extends not only to cover our sins, but also to provide for our emotional and physical needs as well.

Because God is merciful, He comforts his children in their troubles (2 Corinthians 1:4). Here Paul has in mind primarily the hardships one may face for living the Christian life. This hardship may come from religious authorities, governments, families, and so forth. No matter the circmnstances we face, God provides the comfort that is needed so that we might be able to comfort others. So how should we respond to such a blessing? Understand that "just as the sufferings of Christ flow over into our lives, so also through Christ our comfort overflows" (2 Corinthians 1:5).

Conclusion

1 Peter has been called the "handbook on Christian suffering." In this profound letter, the apostle Peter writes to those who are in need of encouragement because of negative external circumstances they are facing. Regarding this need, Peter naturally thinks of God's mercy through Jesus Christ

> Praise be to the God and Father of our Lord Jesus Christ! In his great mercy he has given us new birth into a living hope through the resurrection of Jesus Christ from the dead, and into an inheritance that can never perish, spoil or fade—kept in heaven for you, who through faith are shielded by God's power until the

coming of the salvation that is ready to be revealed in the last time (1 Peter 1:3–5).

We all face hardships, struggles, temptations, and many other difficult things as part of our common human condition. We trust that we can rely on our merciful God in the midst of these difficulties, with the result being a "faith— of greater worth than gold, which perishes even though refined by fire." This faith "may be proved genuine and may result in praise, glory and honor when Jesus Christ is revealed," because "though you have not seen him, you love him; and even though you do not see him now, you believe in him and are filled with an inexpressible and glorious joy, for you are receiving the goal of your faith, the salvation of your souls" (1 Peter 1:7–9). As we come to a greater understanding of God's mercy, our confidence is that God will provide mercy, peace, and love for us in abundance (Jude 2). "Grace, mercy and peace from God the Father and from Jesus Christ, the Father's Son, will be with us in truth and love" (2 John 3).

Questions for Thought and Discussion

1. How does the Bible illustrate man's need for mercy? What examples clearly show our desire for mercy?
2. What are some different types or facets of mercy? Which do we desire from God and from others?

3. How do Old Testament prophecies prove the mercies of God?
4. How was Jesus different in His mercy from previous high priests? Why was He different?
5. Why is mercy to others such an important part of Christianity?

I AM Good

Edmon L. Gallagher

G od's goodness is an important and fundamental doctrine to the understanding of God and of Christianity. As Christians, we gladly serve our God because He is good to us. He has created the world in which we live, given life to our bodies, provided for our daily needs, and desires a relationship with each of us. Even when we are not good, God is always good.

God shows himself to be good in creation. The Bible states that God created the universe (Genesis 1:1). Then God created humans and put them in charge of His world to maintain it (Genesis 1:28). God created both men and women so that they would also have suitable companions (Genesis 1:27; 2:21–22). After He had made everything, God said that it was all '"very good" (Genesis 1:31). Furthermore, the reason God created the universe was for His pleasure and to provide a place for humans to live.

Why would God do that for us? The Bible says plainly that "God is love" (1 John 4:8). Human beings are unique among God's creatures because He made us in His own image—He made us to be like Him (Genesis 1:27). Therefore, He loves us above all other things and He seeks our good. By providing us with food, shelter, and companionship, He proves Himself to be good to us.

If God is good, then why is there so much evil in the world today? The world is no longer as good as when God created it. The Bible states that God has the ability to control the behavior of human beings, but He chooses not to do so. God desires for humans to make good decisions, but He loves us so much that He allows us the freedom to make bad ones. We all know that humans frequently abuse this privilege because of selfishness and the power of sin in our lives. People very often make bad decisions with terrible consequences.

The first bad decision we read about in the Bible comes in the third chapter of Genesis. God had placed Adam and Eve, the first husband and wife, in a garden paradise. Here, all of their needs were met by the God who created them. He gave them one simple rule—"from the tree of the knowledge of good and evil you shall not eat, for in the day that you eat from it you will surely die" (Genesis 2:17). But the man and woman both craved the tree's fruit, and they ate (Genesis 3:6). This disobedience brought down God's curse, not only on the man and woman, but even upon the earth itself. Whereas the soil formerly yielded produce for humanity easily and in abundance, henceforth people would be able to cultivate the land only through much hardship (Genesis 3:17–19; Romans 8:19–22). Thus, evil entered the world through human disobedience or sin.

However, we should be careful not to attribute all the

hardship faced by a person to sinfulness in that person's life. The Bible provides two great examples that overturn any such conclusion. First, the biblical Book of Job encompasses a lengthy conversation between a suffering man and his friends over the causes of his suffering. The friends say that Job is suffering because of the bad decisions he has made and his own sin. Job refuses to accept this, asserting that he has done nothing to deserve his present situation. Job is right, as God declares at the end of the book. It was not Job's personal sin that led to the devastating events of his life—rather, Job's trials gave him the opportunity to exhibit his righteousness in a way that he could not have done otherwise.

The second story comes in the New Testament in the Gospel of John. Chapter nine begins with these words:

> As Jesus walked along, he saw a man blind from birth. His disciples asked him, "Teacher, who sinned, this man or his parents, that he was born blind?" Jesus answered, "Neither this man nor his parents sinned; he was born blind so that God's works might be revealed in him" (1–3),

Here, Jesus clearly declares that this man's physical condition had nothing to do with his spiritual condition but was instead the result of God's plan for him. The story continues by saying that Jesus healed the man, who then became a great witness to the power of God.

The narratives of Job and the blind man whom Jesus healed demonstrate that the suffering we each endure in our lives is not necessarily the result of our own sinfulness.

Nevertheless, we have already seen that it was human sinfulness that brought suffering and hardship into the world in the beginning. Sometimes we do bring difficulty upon ourselves through bad decisions; sometimes we suffer as a result of the sins of others; and sometimes we cannot attribute our suffering to any human cause, but it arises naturally in the form of disease or weather disasters. An example of this would be the terrible tsunami that struck the coasts of India and several other nations around the Bay of Bengal and the Indian Ocean. This natural catastrophe was not caused by God to harm people, but arose naturally through an earthquake shifting the earth's plates. All of this, even the tsunami, ultimately derives from the curse brought on the world following the initial sin as described in Genesis 3.

We did not consider earlier the one who enticed the man and woman to eat the fruit forbidden them by God. The first part of Genesis 3 states that a snake/serpent, representing an agent of evil, spoke to Eve and praised the alluring qualities of the forbidden fruit. The New Testament book of Revelation (12:9) further associates this snake of Genesis with Satan, the great enemy and adversary of God who was an angel (angel means messenger) of God before pride led him to rebel against his maker. Satan's mission now is to lead as many people as possible away from God to join his rebel alliance.

The role of the serpent, as an agent of evil, did not go unnoticed when God cursed the man and woman for their disobedience. Indeed God curses the serpent first, in these words:

The LORD God said to the serpent, "Because you have done this, cursed are you among all animals and among all wild creatures; upon your belly you shall go, and dust you shall eat all the days of your life. I will put enmity between you and the woman, and between your offspring and hers; he will strike your head, and you will strike his heel" (Genesis 3:14–15).

The last part of this curse applies not only to the snake, but is really intended to be understood as applying to Satan. Humans do try to protect themselves from snakes by crushing their heads with their foot or heel, while snakes try to harm humans by biting them on the foot. Literally, this is the meaning of "he will strike your head, and you will strike his heel." But more profoundly, this passage of Scripture lets us know that ultimately, God through humans would defeat every agent of evil, allowing humans to live forever with Him, while destroying evil and death. To be more specific, there is also in this curse a prediction of a coming Savior, Jesus Christ, the "offspring of a woman" who would definitively destroy Satan's power. Here, in the Garden, the scene of man's first disobedience, God was already setting into motion the means by which he would remove all sin and bless humans. God is good.

Because of God's goodness and love for humans, He designed a world that would meet our needs. The flaws now seen in God's creation are not due to any flaws in the original creation, but have come through the curse that resulted from humanity's rebellion against God. It is a testimony to the goodness of God and the power of His creation that the world still serves us as well as it does.

God still sends rain upon the earth and causes vegetation to sprout up to feed both humans and beasts. He allows scientists to discover some of the secrets of the universe in order to improve the lives of people. When Jesus was on the earth, He spoke of God's care for the world and its inhabitants: "Are not two sparrows sold for a cent? And yet not one of them will fall to the ground apart from your Father. But the very hairs of your head are all numbered. So do not fear; you are more valuable than many sparrows" (Matthew 10:29–31). We see here not only that God is our Father, but also that He is concerned about our welfare. Just as He provides for the birds of the air and the beasts of the field, He provides for us as well (Matthew 6:25–34).

God's goodness and care for us is not simply in establishing the world and allowing it to meet our needs naturally. Christians also speak of God's providence. To write it more plainly, "providence" is the mysterious way in which He works in our lives for our good. Providence is mysterious because it is difficult for us to understand how life's events benefit us at the time that we encounter them. Usually, it is only when we can look back on our lives that we can see God's guidance even during troubling times. Jesus said of the blind man that his disability had been prepared by God for the time when God would use him to reveal divine power (John 9:3). The blind man did not understand why he was blind at the time, but after Jesus healed him he confessed faith in God (John 9:38). God had a plan for this blind man, and God's plan involved a much better life than the man ever imagined. In the same way, God has a plan for each of our lives, for our own good, and it is through providence that God enacts His plan in the lives of those who believe in Him.

A great example of God's providence in the Bible is at the end of the book of Genesis in the story of Joseph. Earlier in Genesis, God chose Abraham as the one through whom God's blessing would come to the world, and this would involve increasing Abraham's descendants so that they would become a great nation (Genesis 12:1–3). This began to happen when Abraham's grandson Jacob (who was also known as Israel) had twelve sons, Joseph being the second youngest (Genesis 29:31–30:24; 35:16–18). The last fourteen chapters of Genesis (except chapter 38) concentrate almost exclusively on the life of Joseph and how God used him to bless the world.

The beginning of the story (Genesis 37) gives no indication that God had a special plan for Joseph, except in Joseph's dreams. The young man Joseph tells his parents and brothers that be had dreamed about being out in the field with his family binding sheaves of grain. He continues: "My sheaf rose up and also stood erect; and your sheaves gathered around and bowed down to my sheaf" (Genesis 37:7). Joseph also had another dream: "The sun and the moon and eleven stars were bowing down to me" (Genesis 37:9). His family interpreted these dreams as if Joseph was going to rule over them and they would have to bow down to him. This angered his older brothers, and they determined to get rid of him. They decided not to kill him, but to sell him as a slave instead, and in this way Joseph entered Egypt (Genesis 37:18–36).

In Egypt, Joseph was sold to a man named Potiphar, a high-ranking official of Egypt's king or Pharaoh. It is at such times that people tend to think that God is absent or does not care about us. On the contrary, the Bible says, "The LORD was with Joseph" (Genesis 39:2). We do not know if Joseph realized how involved God was in his life, but we do know that Joseph continued to serve God and God continued to bless Joseph. He became Potiphar's most trusted servant and was put in charge of his entire household. Nevertheless, adversity was not far away. Potiphar's wife desired a sexual relationship with Joseph, but he was too faithful a servant to submit to her attempts to seduce him. She made constant sexual advances toward Joseph, but Joseph always escaped her presence. On one occasion, her advances were very strong and deliberate, and Joseph attempted to escape while she held on to his clothing, forcing Joseph to leave her without being able to escape with all of his clothing. After he fled from her, she lied to her husband, reporting that Joseph had tried to rape her. Potiphar responded by having Joseph imprisoned (Genesis 39:7–20).

Still, the Bible does not allow us to think that God has forgotten about Joseph. "But the LORD was with Joseph and extended kindness to him, and gave him favor in the sight of the chief jailer" (Genesis 39:21). And again, whether or not Joseph understood God's plan for him, even in prison he lived his life faithfully and God blessed him for it. Now in prison, Joseph distinguished himself and became the most trusted prisoner, so that he was put in charge of the other prisoners (Genesis 39:22–23). And in prison Joseph had the opportunity for a blessing that he did not have previously. For it was in prison that he met some fellow prisoners, one of whom had been the cupbearer to Pharaoh, the other having been Pharaoh's baker. Here, God endowed Joseph with the ability to interpret the visions and dreams of the cupbearer and baker (Genesis 40). Joseph predicted that God would restore the cupbearer to his former position before the Pharaoh, while the baker would be put to death by the Pharaoh. Joseph's predictions were true! Soon afterward, the cupbearer was released from prison and resumed his former employment, while the baker was executed. Some time later, Pharaoh had a curious dream one night, and the cupbearer remembered how Joseph had interpreted his dream. Therefore, the cupbearer decided to tell the king that there was a man in prison, by the name of Joseph, who could interpret dreams. The Pharaoh wanted to meet this Joseph. With the help of God, Joseph interpreted the Pharaoh's dream, and the Pharaoh was so impressed by the young man that he made him second-in-command of the entire kingdom.

The time that Joseph spent abused by his family, a slave to Potiphar, and a prisoner in Egypt prepared him for the great responsibility now before him. God had raised him up to the highest levels of earthly authority, but God was still not finished working in Joseph's life. Joseph's main task was to build up a supply of grain in preparation for the extensive famine that they knew was coming to Egypt. Therefore, when everyone in the world needed food, Joseph ensured that Egypt had the food to sell. Eventually, Joseph's brothers made their way to Egypt for food, and they bowed down before their brother Joseph, whom they did not recognize or expect to see (Genesis 42). Soon afterward, Joseph forgives his brothers and is reconciled to them, and Joseph's father, along with his family, move to Egypt to live under the protection of Joseph (Genesis 46).

Throughout his life, God was carrying out His plan for Joseph. Joseph certainly understood God's goodness once he had risen to great power, but he could also see God's goodness as he looked back on his earlier suffering. The story concluded with Joseph telling his brothers, "As for you, you meant evil against me, but God meant it for good in order to bring about this present result, to preserve many people alive" (Genesis 50:20). God used Joseph, even Joseph's sufferings, to save many lived during the famine. God is good.

God is able to bless us fully, as He wants to, when we submit ourselves to Him and allow Him to use us. We have already seen, however, that God has given us the power to resist, and often we do refuse His blessings. Continuing to look at the story in Egypt, we can consider the example of a Pharaoh that lived several hundred years after the time of Joseph. By this time, Jacob's (or Israel's) descendants had become known as Hebrews or as the children of Israel, and they had grown very numerous as God had promised. The Egyptians were fearful of the children of Israel's power and so they forced them into slavery (Exodus 1). God appointed Moses to lead these Hebrews out of Egypt to a new land. Moses approached the Pharaoh about releasing the Hebrew slaves, and told him that God wanted the Hebrews to leave Egypt. The Pharaoh could have submitted to God and released the Hebrews. If he had done so, God had the power to richly bless the Pharaoh for such obedience. Instead, the Pharaoh responded, "Who is the Lord that I should obey His voice to let Israel go? I do not know the LORD, and I will not let Israel go" (Exodus 5:2). The subsequent events humiliated Pharaoh and all of Egypt, and Israel did leave Egypt through God's power.

So, we see in the stories of Joseph and the later Pharaoh that God wants to bless all of our lives, but He allows us to choose whether we will receive His blessing. He does not promise us wealth or greatness, but He does promise to care for our needs if we love Him. Jesus said in the Gospel of Matthew that if we make God the focus of our lives, God will provide for our daily needs when He states, "but seek ye first the kingdom of God and his righteousness, and all these things shall be added unto you" (6:33). The Apostle Paul told the church in Philippi that because of their generosity, God would "supply all your needs according to His riches in glory in Christ Jesus" (Philippians 4:19). Paul himself gave up everything he had for God, but it was his service to God that sustained him throughout his times of adversity, and he never lacked the basic necessities of life (Philippians 4:10–13).

God is good to those who love Him, but He is good also to His enemies. Jesus explained this by saying that God sends rain and sunshine on those who love Him and those who hate Him (Matthew 5:45). At a more profound level, we learn from what the Apostle Paul told the Christians at Rome that "while we were yet enemies" because of our rebellious ways toward God, God still provided for our eternal salvation (Romans 5:10). It is in Jesus Christ that sin's curse is removed from those who are willing to accept the blessing. Jesus Christ is the one who finally has crushed Satan's head, destroyed the power of sin, and revealed the true abundance of God's goodness. Yet, our LORD Jesus did all this through pain and suffering.

God made His love for us known when Jesus Christ came to earth as a man. Through this event, God fully identified with His creatures by becoming one of them. Jesus was not born in a grand palace, but in a barn. He was not a king's son, but the son of a poor working man. Though he went about doing good (Acts 10:38), He did not have a nice house, or even a regular bed (Matthew 8:20). His friends were the outcasts, the poor, the widows, and those with diseases. He affected people and changed the world, not by power and wealth, but by His love for others and His example of righteousness.

A typical example of the goodness that Jesus displayed comes at the very beginning of His ministry in Israel. Very briefly the story is told that a leper approached Jesus asking for help. This was very bold on the part of the leper, because people naturally did not want to encounter leprosy, and lepers were social outcasts. But instead of treating this man as an outcast, Jesus reached out His hand and touched him. The leper professed his faith in Jesus, and Jesus announced that he would be healed from his leprosy. He was immediately healed (Mark 1:40–42).

Jesus did not come to the earth just to show kindness to those unaccustomed to it. He also came to provide a way of eternal salvation from sin for all. He said that He "Did not come to be served, but to serve, and to give his life as a ransom for many" (Matthew 20:28). Jesus sacrificed His life in order to wipe out the sine that humans brought into the world. He did this because of His love for us (John 3:16), and because it is His pleasure to be good toward us.

God's goodness is displayed all around us. He created the world for us to live in it. He provides us with all the necessities of life, whether we are His servants or not. Even in the midst of our hardships, He wants to use us to bless ourselves and others. But most importantly, He calls us to live a life free from sin and one in which we share His goodness with the people around us. It is our choice whether we accept God's goodness, but whatever our decision about God may be, that does not change the fact that God is good!

Questions for Thought and Discussion

1. Does the evil state of the world prove that God is not completely good? Why or why not?
2. Was God the instrument through whom suffering entered the world? Who or what was?
3. In what ways does the providence of God work in our lives today?
4. How does the story of Joseph illustrate the goodness and providence of God?
5. How does God show His goodness even to those who do not believe in Him?

I AM Holy

Kevin J. Youngblood

The Christian Bible repeatedly raises a question that may well be the most important question ever asked. It is a question that opens the door to God's character, to the essence of His divinity. It is a question that points to the one quality underlying all other qualities of God—His holiness. The question is "Who is like God?"

The first time this question is raised is right after God divided the Red Sea and led Israel across it on dry land, after which He closed the sea back up right on top of the Egyptian army. Overwhelmed at such a magnificent deliverance, Israel broke out into spontaneous singing. One of the lines from that first national Hebrew hymn is preserved in Exodus 15:11.

> Who is like you, O LORD, among the gods? Who is like you, majestic in holiness, awesome in glorious deeds, doing wonders?

After this question was first raised at the crossing of the Red Sea, it was repeated again and again in Israel's worship. It is as though this very question defined Israel's worship; it inspired their worship. We hear it again in Psalm 71:19 and 113:5:

Your righteousness, o God, reaches the high heavens. You who have done great things, O God, who is like you? (Psalm 71:9)

Who is like the LORD our God, who is seated on high? (Psalm 113:5)

God Himself raises the question in Isaiah 44:6–7.

Thus says the LORD, the King of Israel and his Redeemer, the LORD of hosts: "I am the first and I am the last; besides me there is no god. Who is like me? Let him proclaim it. Let him declare and set it before me, since I appointed an ancient people. Let them declare what is to come, and what will happen."

He raises it again in Jeremiah 49:14 and 50:44. But nowhere is the question more beautifully stated than in Micah 7:18: "Who is a God like you, pardoning iniquity and passing over transgression for the remnant of his inheritance? He does not retain his anger forever, because he delights in steadfast love." God raises the same basic question in Isaiah 40:25 and 46:5, though in a slightly different form: "'To whom then will you compare me, that I should be like him?' says the Holy One. 'To whom will you liken me and make me equal, and compare me, that we may be alike?'"

That question resurfaces in Scripture over and over again. It is never really answered. Certainly no one offers any examples of someone comparable to God. The question just hangs there. Does it hang there without answer because it is a rhetorical question? Perhaps. Does it hang there without answer because the question is understood to answer itself? Perhaps. I think, however, that the main reason the question just hangs there, hangs there like a challenge, like a dare (I dare you to compare Me to anything) is that words are inadequate to answer the question. The question can only be answered by God's people experiencing over and over again His total uniqueness, by witnessing His incomparable glory and power in their lives.

No one is like God. To say that God is holy is to say that He is without peer, even without analogy. It is to say that we are completely dependent on God's gracious revealing of Himself to know anything about God. God defines Himself by His own words and His own actions. He does not allow anything outside of Himself to define Him. God is not answerable to anything or anyone outside of Himself God cannot be measured by any standard outside of Himself. That is what the holiness of God means, and that is what the question "Who is like God?" invites us to consider.

Rather than define holiness, the biblical story demonstrates it through the way God relates to creation and in particular the way He relates to humans. A good example of the Bible's demonstration of God's holiness is Exodus 3.

In this story, God appears as a burning bush to a man named Moses in order to commission him to liberate a group of slaves that God will turn into a great nation with which He desires to have a special relationship. We will focus especially on Exodus 3:1–12.

Now Moses was keeping the flock of his father-in-law, Jethro, the priest of Midian, and he led his flock to the west side of the wilderness and came to Horeb, the mountain of God. And the angel of the LORD appeared to him in a flame of fire out of the midst of a bush. He looked, and behold, the bush was burning, yet it was not consumed. And Moses said, "I will turn aside to see this great sight, why the bush is not burned." When the LORD saw that he turned aside to see, God called to him out of the bush, "Moses, Moses!" And he said, "Here I am." Then he said, "Do not come near; take your sandals off your feet, for the place on which you are standing is holy ground." And he said, "I am the God of your father, the God of Abraham, the God of Isaac, and the God of Jacob." And Moses hid his face, for he was afraid to look at God. Then the LORD said, "I have surely seen the affliction of my people who are in Egypt and have heard their cry because of their taskmasters. I know their sufferings, and I have come down to deliver them out of the hand of the Egyptians and to bring them up out of that land to a good and broad land, a land flowing with milk and honey, to the place of the Canaanites, the Hittites, the Amorites, the Perizzites, the Hivites, and the Jebusites. And now, behold, the cry of the people of Israel has come to me, and I have also seen the oppression with which the Egyptians oppress them. Come, I will send you to Pharaoh that you may bring my people, the children of Israel, out of Egypt." But Moses said to God, "Who am I that I should go to Pharaoh and bring the children of Israel out of Egypt?" He said, "But I will be with you, and this shall be the sign for you, that I have sent you: when you have brought the people out of Egypt, you shall serve God on this mountain."

I want to focus particularly on the way God reveals Himself to Moses. Why does God reveal Himself as a burning bush? Why does God choose to reveal Himself as a fire, a fire that burns but without destroying? I used to think that the burning bush was just a way of directing Moses's attention to God. Upon further reflection, however, I have come to realize that God was actually saying something substantive about Himself through that apparition. In fact, this image of God as a fire resting in a bush but not consuming it reveals the very heart of holiness.

The first thing to notice about this fire is that it was not dependent on the bush for its existence. Normally, fires require fuel to burn, and once they use up all of their fuel they die out. Not this fire. This fire burned without using any of the bush's energy. The bush contributed nothing to the fire; the fire was completely self-sustaining. The fire resided in the bush not because it had to but because it wanted to. Divine holiness is God's complete independence, His total self-sufficiency, and self-reliance. In other words, God has need of nothing outside of Himself. He is completely distinct from His creation. He is not trapped inside of it, or dissolved into it, or even dependent on it.

At first, the statement "God doesn't need you" may sound condescending. But think about it again. Think about what that means. That means that God has no ulterior motives in seeking a relationship with us. He seeks a relationship with us out of sheer love, pure unselfish desire to share the eternal, holy love of the Father, Son, and Spirit. The divine covenant, whether old or new, is not a relationship of two equals, God on the one hand and humans on the other. It is not God coming to us saying, "Well, we need each other in order to survive so let's enter into a relationship." God's holy love is never so pragmatic, self-serving, and unromantic. When God seeks a relationship with us, it is purely for our benefit and well-being, not out of any need He has. It is God's holiness (His independence from anything or anyone outside of Himself) that makes His love so radically other-centered, so selfless, and pure. Because God doesn't need us, He is able to enjoy freely loving us regardless of our response.

This also means that God's power comes from outside the created realm. He is entirely distinct from creation, and therefore bears none of the corruption or limitations of the fallen creation. This is precisely why God alone is able to do something about the mess we have made of our lives and His world. He is outside of the problem and therefore can reach in and pull us out.

The second thing to notice about the fire is that, contrary to the nature of fire, it did not destroy the bush! Fire and dry underbrush are a dangerous combination. Yet God created a fire that left the bush intact and alive. In this way God communicates precisely the kind of relationship He is forming with His people. Despite the fact that sin has turned us completely inward and made us selfish, and has tainted our every attempt at love with self-serving, ulterior motives, God desires to be with us, even to live in our midst.

The question is: How can He do that without lowering His standards? How can He dwell in our midst with His intolerance of evil without destroying us for our complicity in evil and our participation in corrupting the world that He made and loves? One would think that the only options left for a holy God after our thorough corruption in sin would be either separation or destruction. He must either permanently separate Himself from us or He must vent the full fury of holy wrath that sin deserves and annihilate us. God refuses both options. He refuses to be placed in that kind of dilemma. He finds a third way. He will gently and gradually infuse us with His holiness. By living in an intimate relationship with us, and atoning for our sins through blood sacrifice, God will eventually make us holy like Himself. But He will do so in a way that does not destroy us, that preserves our willing participation in the process, as painstakingly slow as that may be.

The only explanation for the bush's surviving the flames is that somehow it must have partaken of the fire's own properties, of the fire's own power and purity. It must have exchanged the quality of combustion for the fire's quality of consecration. One thing that the burning bush communicates very powerfully is that it is a profound miracle to live in the divine presence, to be with Him and worship Him, and to survive the experience! The only reason we survive worship is because in it He is transforming us into His holy likeness.

In this sense, the burning bush foreshadows the tabernacle, the construction of which occupies a full fourth of the book of Exodus (instructions 25-31; constructions 35:30–40:38). The tabernacle was God's tent in which He dwelled as a holy fire, purifying the people of Israel through atonement and communion. The tabernacle represented the presence of the vagabond God of a vagabond people, content to live in a tent in the middle of a harsh desert if that is what it takes to be with His people and to influence them toward holiness.

This leads us to a third consideration regarding the way God defines His own holiness. Having communicated to Moses through the burning bush His intent to dwell among His people and make them holy, God proceeds to share with Moses His sensitivity to His people's suffering. Twice our text emphasizes how profoundly aware God is that His people are hurting, suffering under the weight of oppression, victimized by the sin and selfishness of others. God communicates this concern in Exodus 2:23–25 and 3:7–8:

> During those many days the king of Egypt died, and the people of Israel groaned because of their slavery and cried out for help. Their cry for rescue from slavery came up to God. And God heard their groaning, and God remembered his covenant with Abraham, with Isaac, and with Jacob. God saw the people of Israel—and God knew.
>
> Then the LORD said, "I have surely seen the afflic-

tion of my people who are in Egypt and have heard their cry because of their taskmasters. I know their sufferings, and I have come down to deliver them out of the hand of the Egyptians and to bring them up out of that land to a good and broad land, a land flowing with milk and honey, to the place of the Canaanites, the Hittites, the Amorites, the Perizzites, the Hivites, and the Jebusites. And now, behold, the cry of the people of Israel has come to me, and I have also seen the oppression with which the Egyptians oppress them. Come, I will send you to Pharaoh that you may bring my people, the children of Israel, out of Egypt."

In fact, God's awareness of His people's pain moves beyond mere observation and into actual participation. God says that not only had He observed their oppression but He had "known" it—a Hebrew idiom which in this context means He had "felt" it.

This speaks profoundly to one of the greatest misconceptions of holiness. We tend to think of holiness only in terms of separation. While, indeed, as we have already discussed, holiness does involve God's radical independence and His existence outside of the created order, it also involves interaction. Holiness is not separation for separation's sake. Holiness is separation for the sake of purified involvement. God, in His holiness, separates Himself from suffering so that He can enter it voluntarily and destroy suffering from within. God's holy sense of Israel's pain moves Him to descend into their situation and to bring relief with Him (v. 8). God defines holiness as a sensitivity to evil, a sensitivity to the suffering of others that motivates purified involvement—that is an involvement that originates from outside the situation and voluntarily enters the situation with the power of relief.

This notion of purified involvement leads to the fourth consideration of God's definition of holiness. Notice that as Moses approached the burning bush to take a closer look God immediately spoke to him, commanding him to come no closer and to remove his shoes because the ground on which he stood was holy (3:5–6). If it is in fact the case, as the burning bush indicates, that God wants to be near His people, why does He demand that they keep their distance? This is true not only of Moses's encounter with God at the burning bush, but also of Israel after her deliverance from bondage at the hand of Moses. When these rescued slaves gathered around Mt. Sinai to meet for the first time the holy God who delivered them, He warns them not to touch the mountain on which He appeared to them lest they die.

> The LORD said to Moses, "Go to the people and consecrate them today and tomorrow, and let them wash their garments and be ready for the third day." For on the third day the LORD will come down on Mount Sinai in the sight of all the people. "And you shall set limits for the people all around, saying, 'Take care not to go up into the mountain or touch the edge of it. Whoever touches the mountain shall be put to death'" (Exodus 19:10–12).

How does this distance that God creates between Himself and His people contribute to the close relationship He seeks to have with us? The answer is that intimacy with God is only possible through His approaching us. The chasm between ourselves and God can only be closed from His side. Any attempt we make to move toward Him on our own terms or on our own initiative inevitably leads to our destruction.

God says to us, "Stay where you are, and I will find you. If you try to find me you will only grow more confused, more disoriented, and more lost." I remember one time when I went to the market to buy food with my mother and I got lost. I was so absorbed in looking at all the delicious food that I failed to notice that my mother had moved on to another booth. I looked up from my daydreaming to find myself surrounded by strangers. I panicked and began running everywhere desperately looking for my mother. She had only been a short distance away, but at the end of my crazed attempt to find her I was at the opposite end of the market. Finally I gave up and crumpled to the ground in tears.

Several minutes later my mother found me, but I had prolonged our reunion by trying to find her my way. I will never forget what she said to me. She said, "Kevin, always remember when you get lost, just stay where you are and I will find you. The market place is no place for a little boy to be wandering around." We had talked about it before, but I panicked and tried to find her my way instead of her way. That is why God does not want us to touch His mountain. He is coming down to us and does not want us trying to find our own way up to Him. That can only lead to being more desperately lost than we were before.

It is not for humans to approach God uninvited. We must never make the mistake of thinking that God is on the same continuum we are on and that if we just keep moving along this continuum we will eventually catch up with Him. God is not just ahead of us in some evolutionary process. He is not just an advanced, or even perfected version of ourselves. He is something else altogether, and He must define how we relate to Him.

One of the reasons I believe God appeared to Israel as a storm on Mt. Sinai is because storms are beyond our control. We cannot predict them, control them, or capture them. God is like that. He is not subject to human manipulation. We can never figure Him out. He cannot be bribed or bargained with. More importantly, He does not need to be bribed or bargained with. He loves you with a holy love and wants to be with you, but that can only happen when He comes to you.

And God did come to us. He came to us in the person of Jesus Christ. The holiness of God was wrapped in the flesh and blood of Jesus. God did this for two reasons. The first is so that we could understand His holiness by seeing it modeled in human form. Jesus's purity from sin, His concern for people, His involvement with the poor, and suffering to bring relief all pointed to the holiness of God. This is what Jesus meant when He said in Matthew 11:27, "All things have been handed over to me by my Father and no one knows the Son except the Father, and no one knows the Father except the Son and those to whom the Son chooses to reveal Him." Jesus chose to reveal the holiness of God by modeling it in His own behavior.

The second reason God came to us in all of His holiness in the person of Jesus is so that we could share in His holiness. God wants to make us holy by entering into a relationship with us by which He can influence us and infuse us with His own holy character. Jesus was the perfect example of this kind of relationship and the one through whom every other human has the opportunity to experience this relationship. Though the holiness of God necessarily means that He is fundamentally unlike us and unlike anything we know, it does not mean that He is unapproachable or unknowable. In fact, God's holiness radiates outward and makes holy anyone who wishes to have a relationship with God through faith in Christ. This is why God says in the Bible, "Be holy for I am holy" (Leviticus 19:2).

Holiness is the tension between God's separation from His creatures and His involvement with them. This tension is perfectly expressed by God through the prophet Isaiah:

> For thus says the One who is high and lifted up, who inhabits eternity, whose name is Holy: "I dwell in the high and holy place, and also with him who is of a contrite and lowly spirit, to revive the spirit of the lowly, and to revive the heart of the contrite" (Isaiah 57:15).

Questions for Thought and Discussion

1. Why is it impossible to answer the question, "Who is like God?"
2. Why does God choose a burning bush to reveal Himself to Moses?

3. How does God's lack of need for us actually serve as a proof of His love for us?
4. Does the concept of holiness only imply a separation from God? Why or why not?
5. In what ways did Jesus exemplify holiness?

I AM Just

Cory Collins

"The Rock! His work is perfect, for all His ways are just; a God of faithfulness and without injustice, righteous and upright is He." These are words stated by the prophet of God, Moses, in Deuteronomy 32:4.

The Meaning of the Word "Just"

Defining the word "just" will help clarify this important aspect of the nature of God. "Just" signifies "honorable and fair in one's dealings and actions," as when we speak of a just ruler who treats all subjects impartially under the law. "Just" means "consistent with what is morally right; righteous," as when we speak of a just cause which is intended to rectify unfair conditions. "Just" means "based on fact or sound reason; well-founded," as when we speak of a just appraisal of a diamond or a piece of property.

God: Perfectly Just

These qualities, which we admire and appreciate in people, originate with God and reflect His character. He demonstrates them perfectly. God always acts in accordance with what is right and cannot do otherwise. In addition to that, God Himself is the final standard or criterion of what is right.

In other words, God has not arbitrarily decided what is right and what is wrong. It is not as if He chose to prohibit and punish certain things while commanding and rewarding others. Rather, right and wrong are inseparably tied to God's very essence. Whatever fits God's nature is right; whatever violates God's nature is wrong. There is not some standard above God, to which He must submit. There is no external law which rules over God's decisions. Rather, the standard is within God.

It is different with a human judge. When a judge hears a case in court, the judge must decide that case based upon the law which he has promised to uphold, and this is a law which was learned from instructors who explained it to the judge. Whenever necessary the judge consults books for examples of past cases that will help clarify his or her approach to the matter at hand. However, the judge is not the author who wrote the law, but one who is merely the agent who upholds the law.

On the other hand, God is both the author and the agent of what is truly just. He originated justice. He demonstrates justice. He declares justice. He demands justice. When God tells us in the Bible what is just and what is unjust, He is telling us who He is and teaching us to think, speak, and act as He does.

For example, God has declared that lying is sinful. Why? The reason is that God Himself is true in all His ways, words, and works. God cannot lie, as Titus 1:2 notes. Lying contradicts God's character. God could no more lie than He could die. When He forbids us to lie, He is not only saying that lying is unjust, though it is. He is saying that we are to imitate Him and that lying keeps us from doing that.

In a similar way the Bible teaches us not to steal, but to give and to share. It commands us to be faithful to our promises and our marriages. It challenges us to love our enemies. It tells us to defend and protect the widow and the orphan. In all these matters the Scriptures are exhorting us to live according to what is just in the sight of, and in the nature of, God.

By inspiration the prophet Micah wrote: "He has told you, O man, what is good; and what does the LORD require of you but to do justice, to love kindness, and to walk humbly with your God" (Micah 6:8). We "do justice" by living according to God's definition of what is just. For that reason we "love kindness," offering mercy to those in need. In this way we show that we "walk humbly" with God, following His lead according to His directions in the Bible.

So when one says that God is just, one means that God always acts in accordance with what is right and that God Himself is the final standard of what is right. Because God is a moral Being, and perfect in all His attributes, He is perfectly just.

Humanity's Desire for Justice

God created man in His own image, according to His likeness (Genesis 1:26–27). Therefore, He put within each of us a sense of and a yearning for justice. Even those who have never read the Bible recognize in their hearts that certain behaviors are just or unjust. The Bible says,

> For when Gentiles who do not have the Law do instinctively the things of the Law, these, not having the Law, are a law to themselves, in that they show the work of the Law written in their hearts, their conscience bearing witness, and their thoughts alternately accusing or else defending them, on the day when, according to my gospel, God will judge the secrets of men through Christ Jesus (Romans 2:14–16).

This fact first of all confirms the existence of God, who is personal, fair, and moral. If there were no God, if we had evolved as a result of time plus chance plus accidents, we would not have what we call the conscience. This "built-in" compass, which we use all the time to evaluate whether a situation is just or not, is proof of the fact that we have a marvelous Creator.

Secondly, this fact provides the basis for law and order in society. Since all responsible people agree, for example, that stealing is not just and must be punished, all governments enact laws that reflect this shared understanding. When such laws are passed, no sensible person says, "Wait a minute! Stealing is morally right and should be allowed and encouraged!" The same is true regarding marriage as well. Virtually every culture throughout history has recognized the importance of marriage and has enacted laws to preserve and protect the family.

Of course each of us has a choice as to whether we will follow what we know is right or not. When we sin we violate God's standard which is written both in the Bible and in our hearts. The fact that we know what is just does not guarantee that we will do what is just. Every responsible person has chosen to commit sin at some point. For that reason we need God's forgiveness through the sacrifice of His Son, Jesus Christ. We will discuss this further as we continue this chapter.

First let us notice that we consistently demonstrate this God-given recognition of what is just and what is unjust, because He created all of us in His image. For example, when two opponents appear before a judge and jury in court, we want the result to be fair to all who are involved. We are upset and disappointed if someone bribes the judge with money or destroys the evidence that would contribute to a fair trial.

In a political election, we expect all the votes to be counted. In an athletic contest, we want the rules of fair play to be honored and enforced. When we purchase an item with cash, we count the change to be sure it is correct. We want to see the poor treated with the same respect as the wealthy. We believe that the laws of society must apply equally to all and that those who break such laws must be punished. We become angry when we see injustice and prejudice. We know that the same standard—not a double standard—must be upheld in every case, every dispute, and every contest. What's fair is fair. What's right is right.

The Bible lists attitudes and behaviors that are not just; they are not right in the eyes of God. One who reads such passages with an open mind will agree that the Bible is right, because God has placed these same truths in the hearts of His creatures. For example, the Word of God speaks of people

> ... being filled with all unrighteousness, wickedness, greed, evil; full of envy, murder, strife, deceit, malice; they are gossips, slanderers, haters of God, insolent, arrogant, boastful, inventors of evil, disobedient to parents, without understanding, untrustworthy, unloving, unmerciful; and, although they know the ordinance of God, that those who practice such things are worthy of death, they not only do the same, but also give hearty approval to those who practice them (Romans 1:29–32).

Notice these words: "although they know the ordinance of God." How do people, even without the Bible, know God's verdict? How do they know that certain attitudes and actions are worthy of death? They know—we know — because we are made in the image of God. As a result we understand what is just. We seek what is just. We are free to disobey what is just, knowing that there will be consequences.

Results of God's Justice

Because God is just, He loves all people equally. He does not pick and choose among people based on their wealth, ethnic background, education, gender, age, or ability. He does not look at the outward appearance but at the heart. Simon Peter, one of Jesus's apostles, said: "I most certainly understand now that God is not one to show partiality, but in every nation the man who fears Him and does what is right, is welcome to Him" (Acts 10:34–35). Through the Gospel, God invites every person to come to know Him, regardless of his or her background, nationality, or outward circumstances.

God gives gifts to all people, even those who do not obey Him. Jesus said that " ... your Father in heaven ... causes His sun to rise on the evil and the good, and sends rain on the righteous and the unrighteous" (Matthew 5:45). When the Apostle Paul spoke of God's generosity to all people, he said:

> And in the generations gone by He permitted all the nations to go their own ways; and yet He did not leave Himself without witness, in that He did good and gave you rains from heaven and fruitful seasons, satisfying your hearts with food and gladness (Acts 14:16–17).

Therefore, the Bible teaches us to treat others without prejudice or discrimination. In James 2:1–10 we are warned not to show favoritisim. We must not give higher regard to the rich, or lower regard to the poor. Instead we are to love our neighbors as we love ourselves, though they may be quite differnt from us and from each other. Why? The reason is that God does not discriminate against us based on such outward elements.

There is another side to this truth as well. Because God is just, He applies the same standard to all. Sometime people say, "Justice is blind." They mean by this phrase that everyone must pay the consequences of breaking the law, no matter the person's economic level, educational accomplishments, gender, ethnic background, relationship to the judge, or any other factor. According to the Bible, this is our greatest problem. We have broken God's law by acting contrary to His standard. It was to solve that greatest problem that God provided the greatest solution at the greatest possible cost. He gave His Son, Jesus Christ, to pay the penalty for our sins, satisfy divine justice, and set us free.

The Day of Judgment

Because God is God, He cannot simply look the other way and pretend that sin does not exist. Though He loves us with all His heart, He hates sin with all His heart just as much. As a human judge might feel compassion toward a convict but also be obligated to make him pay for his crime, so it is with God. Every sin must be judged and condemned. Sometimes when a human father has to punish his son or daughter he says, "This is going to hurt me a lot worse than it hurts you!" He means, of course, that he loves his child deeply and punishes him or her only because it is necessary. Yet it is necessary.

God's justice requires that all responsible people appear

before His throne in Heaven and give account on the great Day of Judgment at the end of time. The Apostle Paul declared to the philosophers in Athens, Greece long ago:

> Therefore having overlooked the times of ignorance, God is now declaring to men that all everywhere should repent, because He has fixed a day in which He will judge the world in righteousness through a Man whom He has appointed, having furnished proof to all men by raising Him from the dead (Acts 17:30–31).

Jesus spoke of people from different nations, separated by many centuries, appearing together at the Day of Judgment (Matthew 12:41–42). He said that He Himself would sit on the throne and place people either on His right, to enter Heaven, or on His left, to enter Hell (Matthew 25:31–46).

The penalty for sin is death. The Bible says, "The person who sins will die" (Ezekiel 18:4, 20). It also notes, "The wages of sin is death" (Romans 6:23). The Bible describes a death that is far worse than physical death. It is an eternal separation from God and from all that is good in a place of outer darkness, unquenchable fire, and the weeping and gnashing of teeth.

Jesus was emphatic about this terrifying place of torment called Hell. He spoke of a Day of Judgment in which He would say to some, "Depart from Me, accursed ones, into the eternal fire which has been prepared for the devil and his angel" (Matthew 25:41). He also said that in Hell "their worm does not die, and the fire is not quenched" (Mark 9:48). Jesus spoke as well of those who would be "cast out into outer darkness; there shall be weeping and gnashing of teeth" (Matthew 8:12; 22:13; 25:30).

The Bible teaches that we have but one life upon the earth. We do not have more than one opportunity to live with God. This is contrary to the concept of reincarnation, the belief that one lives many successive lives one earth, perhaps in different forms, as a consequence of *karma* or guilt. Rather it states clearly, "... it is appointed for men to die once, and after this comes judgment ..." (Hebrews 9:27).

The Apostle John wrote:

> Then I saw a great white throne and Him who sat upon it, from whose presence earth and heaven fled away, and no place was found for them. And I saw the dead, the great and the small, standing before the throne, and books were opened; and another book was opened, which is the book of life; and the dead were judged from the things which were written in the books, according to their deeds. And the sea gave up the dead which were in it, and death and Hades gave up the dead which were in them; and they were judged, every one of them according to their deeds. Then death and Hades were thrown into the lake of fire. This is the second death, the lake of fire. And if anyone's name was not found written in the book of life, he was thrown into the lake of fire (Revelation 20:11–15).

God Through the Gospel: Both Just and Justifier

How could God (because of His justice) faithfully punish our sin but (because of His love) legitimately let us go free?

How could God satisfy His righteous wrath but also provide His generous grace? How could God bring sinners to Heaven who deserve to be lost in Hell? This apparent dilemma led to the event which distinguishes Christianity from all other religions of the world: the sacrifice of Jesus Christ.

"For God so loved the world, that He gave His only begotten Son, that whoever believes in Him should not perish, but have eternal life" (John 3:16). God offered His unique Son, Jesus Christ, as a substitute for each of us. Jesus Christ became the scapegoat who paid the debt we owed but could not pay. When He was crucified on a cross 2,000 years ago, He bore our sins in His body (1 Peter 2:24).

This is the Gospel, the "good news." We sinners can be forgiven because of the penalty Jesus Christ paid for our sins! The Bible says: "'He (God the Father) made Him (Jesus Christ the Son) who knew no sin to be sin on our behalf, that we might become the righteousness of God in Him" (2 Corinthians 5:21). In other words, God exchanged Jesus Christ for each of us, so that Jesus became our sin and we became His righteousness.

The Bible likewise describes what Jesus did in these terms:

> ... for all have sinned and fall short of the glory of God, being justified as a gift by His grace through the redemption which is in Christ Jesus; whom God displayed publicly as propitiation in His blood through faith. This was to demonstrate His righteousness, because in the forbearance of God He passed over the sins previously

committed; for the demonstration, I say, of His right-eousness at the present time, that He might be just and the justifier of the one who has faith in Jesus (Romans 3:23–26).

Let's define some of these terms so that we may under-stand them more clearly. "We have sinned" means that we have missed the mark and broken God's just law. "Fall short" signifies that we are unable to reach God by our own efforts, because of the power of sin in our lives. "Justified" suggests "made right with God, as if we had never sinned." "Grace" is a free gift; "redemption" is deliverance from bondage by payment of a ransom price.

"Propitiation" is an appeasement, an offering that satis-fies the offended party. When a person has hurt his friend and then seeks to be reconciled, he may present a gift to that friend. He hopes that, when the friend receives the gift, the friend will be no longer angry, but gracious. In the same way, the offering of Jesus Christ in our place appeases God's righteous demands and allows God to receive us in love.

That is why this Scripture says that, through Jesus Christ, God may be both just and the justifier of the one who has faith in Jesus. God is just because He has justly demanded payment for every sin at His Son's expense. God is the justifier because He is, at the same time, able to make us just in His sight and treat us as if we were right-eous. In other words, God reconciles us or reunites us with Himself through the death of Christ.

Paul the Apostle wrote by inspiration:

For while we were still helpless, at the right time Christ died for the ungodly. For one will hardly die for a righteous man; though perhaps for the good man someone would dare even to die. But God demonstrates His own love toward us, in that while we were yet sinners, Christ died for us. Much more then, having now been justified by His blood, we shall be saved from the wrath of God through Him. For if while we were enemies, we were reconciled to God through the death of His Son, much more, having been reconciled, we shall be saved by His life. And not only this, but we also exult in God through our Lord Jesus Christ, through whom we have now received the reconciliation (Romans 5:6–11).

Becoming Right With God

Though the Gospel is for everyone, and Jesus died for all of us, God requires that we accept the Gospel through obedient faith in order to be justified. Having heard the Gospel, as you have heard it in this lesson, it is important for you to decide whether or not you believe it and whether you are willing to put your trust in God, before you can be saved. You must believe that Jesus Christ is, in fact, the Son of God. You must believe that ". . . Christ died for our sins according to the Scriptures, and that He was buried, and that He was raised on the third day according to the Scriptures ... " (1 Corinthians 15:3–4).

This is not just an internal belief, but something you believe so strongly that you would be willing to tell anyone, whether it be family members, neighbors, or strangers. You must be willing to confess that faith before others. The

Scripture says: "Fight the good fight of faith; take hold of the eternal life to which you were called, and you made the good confession in the presence of many witnesses" (1 Timothy 6:12).

You must, as a part of that faith, repent of your sins. When we acknowledge that God is truly who He says He is, and then means a just God, then we will also feel compelled to make our lives right before Him. That is, you turn from your sinful thoughts and ways. Acknowledging your sin, you know that it grieves God and that it cost the life of His Son, Jesus Christ. You determine that, with God's help, you will no longer practice your former sins.

You must, as an expression of that faith, be baptized (immersed in water) into Jesus Christ for the forgiveness of your sins. The Scripture says: " ... Repent, and let each of you be baptized in the name of Jesus Christ for the forgiveness of your sins; and you shall receive the gift of the Holy Spirit" (Acts 2:38). I ask you this same question, which was asked long ago: "And now why do you delay? Arise, and be baptized, and wash away your sins, calling on His name" (Acts 22:16).

The person who gave you this book will be happy to answer your questions and to assist you. It is our prayer that you will desire to be a Christian, a follower of Jesus Christ.

Questions for Thought and Discussion

1. How is God's judgment different from human judgment?

2. Why is it necessary for God to demand payment for our sins?

3. How do the laws of today's societies show the justice of God?

4. Is it possible for God to change what is just and what is unjust? Why or why not?

5. How can God be both just and justifier? How does He accomplish this without contradicting His nature?

I AM Love

Larry Murdock

There is a prayer that reads:

From the unreal lead me to the real:
From the darkness lead me to light:
From death lead me to immortality.

The unwanted characteristics of unreality, darkness, and death are uniquely experienced by individual persons, even though these trials are common to all. Only the living, loving Godhead can answer this prayer and bring a person's deepest longings to actuality.

As discussed in an earlier chapter, the Godhead is composed of Yahweh (the Father), His Holy Spirit, and His Word (the Son who later became flesh; John 1:14). Out of great love this Godhead created. On the sixth day of creation,

God said; let us make man in our image, after our likeness: and let them have dominion over the fish of the
sea, and over the birds of the heavens, and over the
cattle, and over all the earth, and over every creeping
thing that creeps upon the earth. And God created man
in his own image, in the image of God created he him;
male and female created he them (Genesis 1:26–27).

God created and endowed the human family with reality, light, and immortality.

The eternal God created human uniqueness and
endowed the human spirit with everlasting existence. He
planted living seed with bountiful and fertile DNA in both
the first man and woman so that flesh and spirit could be
united in the same body. God then blessed the first couple
by saying, "be fruitful, and multiply, and fill the earth, and
subdue it" (Genesis 1:28). The couple was created in the
image of God. They were then commanded to bear children. The children also then bore the characteristics of
God. And so God's image was passed along to all
succeeding generations of humans, from the beginning
down to the present.

True love, in whomever it is found, always wishes to
share life. God chose to share His life with humans. The
Bible describes God as the essence of life and states, "the
Life was the light of humans" (John 1:4). God loves humans
—so much that He wanted to share "life" so greatly that it
shined like a great light amongst humans. Indeed, God's
love is so great that He created human beings because God
is Love (1 John 4:7–8).

A Tested Method for Discovering God's Love

There is a proven method by which humans can begin to understand God's great love for humans. The method commands that we reason backwards, from humans back to the Creator. Jesus, Yahweh's only begotten Son, demonstrated this method when He was teaching the goodness of God (Luke 11:9–13). Jesus asked which of those men present would give his son a stone, if the son asked for bread. Which of them would give his son a serpent, if he asked for a fish? Which father among them would give his son a scorpion, if the son asked for an egg? None of those fathers would behave in such a way toward their sons! Jesus drew this conclusion, "if you then being evil, know how to give good gifts to your children, how much more will your heavenly Father give the Holy Spirit to those who ask Him!" Jesus demonstrated the method that humans can learn some things about the heavenly Father by looking at the love of "evil" fathers. Earthly fathers do many things unbecoming of the Creator because they are sinful. Nevertheless, earthly fathers have traits that they inherited from the image of God. Humanity bears God's image in a number of ways! Therefore, we may learn some things about God by this method of looking at man, who was created in the image of God. However, a word of caution is necessary. Because of human sin, this procedure alone must not be the only source of our understanding of God, for fear that we would "create" an image of God patterned only after our own mental image of what we think God would be like. Our human conclusions, then, need God's own collaboration given in His revealed book, the Bible.

The Loving God Desired Children

Why would a man and woman desire children? Why would they wish to recreate their own image or likeness? It is true that some people do not desire children, but most experience a strong desire to have children. And even those people who cannot have children may wish that they could. Desiring children is a divine way to share love, or to extend love; it is no wonder that ideal procreation rests on love in a home where one male and one female love one another emotionally, cogitatively, and physically. In this wonderful union that the Bible calls "one flesh" is found the power to create eternal children. The loving God placed this power within His first human offspring and commanded them to do as He had done within the confines of a committed marital love. Yahweh himself lovingly desired us as His children.

God's Love and a Dwelling Place

Earthly parents want their children to have a dwelling place called "home"; God desires for His offspring a dwelling place. God created the heavens and the earth, and particularly Eden, as a dwelling place for humanity. Everything made in the heavens and earth was made for the existence of humanity. The creatures of the earth are here for humans; the vegetation of earth is here for humans; the challenges of the earth and of civilization are here for humanity. It is humanity's task to go forth subduing the earth and bringing all earthly things into helpful relationship with humanity, modeling their heavenly Father. Even procreation itself has subduing the earth in view (Genesis 1:28).

God's Love and Autonomy

God desires autonomy for His children. Again, think of earthly parents; their desire is to see their beloved children have a healthy, wonderful life of their own, on their own. They want them to be autonomous. Autonomy means fmally giving children complete control of their own lives. Before a child leaves home, his or her will power may lead them to rebel against the parent, but the parent may exercise power to enforce conformity to the parent's own will. However, this is neither desirable nor pleasurable to the parent. It is a hollow victory over the child. The parent would prefer the child to observe and understand the ways of the parent so as to follow the parent's lead and example voluntarily. So likewise, God's desire for His offspring is that they would desire to follow His ways willingly, of their own choosing or free will. God created man and woman to be autonomous because He loves us.

God's Love and Longevity

God desires for His children longevity. We have the heaviest sympathy for those who have lost children or grandchildren. No human father or mother ever wants to outlive their children or grandchildren. How much more so God, who is pure love and wholly eternal (1 John 4:8; Psalm 90:2)? The word "death" means separation. People who have lost children to physical death know, better than any other human can, how God feels about the spiritual death of His children. The Bible teaches that there is spiritual death, and it is worse than physical death!

"Precious in the sight of the LORD is the [physical] death of His saints" (Psalm 116:15). God knows that a man's physical death is just a one time experience. The eternal spirit of humans does not and cannot die or cease to exist, for it is made in the image of the eternal God; but it is possible for us to be spiritually separated from God, which is called the "second death" (Revelation 2:11; 21:8). Humans cope with small "deaths" throughout life; that is, we experience everyday separations and goodbyes. But most of our separations are with hope, that is, the expectation that we will see one another again, perhaps soon! And so, we shoulder our separations fairly easily. But separations that have signs of permanency can cause us great grief. Consider divorce, or a son going off to war, or a family member going on a dangerous mission, or the physical death of one beloved. Knowing then the sadness, heartache, tears, and sorrows associated with death, the loving heavenly Father of all would spare us overmuch sorrow by giving us immortality (1 Thessalonians 4:13; John 16:20).

So God has desired for His children longevity and freedom from an eternal separation (death). In fact, God has made a plan to save His created children from eternal death and give them an eternal home (life) with Him in a place called Heaven (Romans 6:23; Psalm 11:4; 14:2; Matthew 18:10; Revelation 7:17; 21:4).

God's Love and Creative Occupation

The loving God also desires for His children a creative occupation. Every human parent desires a livelihood for his or her children. God, too, gave humans an enormous task of multiplying and filling the earth with created souls. People are supposed to subdue the created world for noble human and godly purposes. The human job description was given to humanity before sin entered the world (Genesis 1:28). Therefore, the "subduing" of the creation does not have reference to overcoming sin or its derivatives such as sorrow, disease, or hardships—things which mankind are likely to associate with the idea of "conquering" the elements of the heavens and the earth. Subduing the creation then must have had reference to the benefits that humans could have creatively extracted from the earth for the continuing genuine human joy and peace of the planet. Since sin entered the creation, new obstacles have made subduing the earth more difficult (Genesis 3:17–19). Therefore, the command to subdue the earth has taken on the idea of conquering the obstacles to human joy and peace that have been produced by sin on a now hostile planet.

God's Love and Walking in His Ways

God also desires His children to walk in His ways, duplicating the thinking and the emotions of Himself; this is called godliness. God envisioned that humanity would live in a beautiful physical world, forever "walking" with Him. God gave His first son and daughter all the opportunities they needed for a walk with Him (Genesis 3:8). He gave them a marvelous body with marvelous abilities, which could be sustained eternally by the fruit from God's tree of life (Genesis 2:8–9). God joined that potentially eternal body with an eternal spirit made in His image that empowered and energized the human body. The energy was called the "breath of life," or spirit; the spirit was breathed into the freshly created body of man so that it became a living soul (Genesis 2:7). Later, God created the woman as man's perfect counterpart (Genesis 2:21–22). God gave the union of male and female the power to create children made in their own image (thus in the image of God), and souls (body and spirit) that would be sustained by God's "tree of life," which would ensure the body's eternal longevity. God also gave His children a beautiful home in which to begin their work of multiplying and subduing all creation. These were the loving desires of God's heart and the purposes that underlay His creation. *The foundation of all these matters is the fact that the very nature of God is Love (1 John 4:8).*

The Sin of the First Parents

God created human beings to be free, but as Adam and Eve learned, God also holds human beings accountable for their choices (Genesis 3:9–19; 2 Corinthians 5:10). Adam and Eve were able to rebel because the loving God had what they will do. Adam and Eve's disobedience has brought humanity to the brink of Hell, which God made for Satan and his demons (Matthew 25:41). When humans followed Satan into sin they brought upon themselves the same eternal punishment reserved for Satan in Hell.

However, the loving heavenly Father of all spirits

(Hebrews 12:9) has revealed His great love for His sinful children by sending to their rescue His only begotten Son, Jesus Christ (Romans 5:8). Since the wages of sin is death, the sinless Jesus came to earth to endure the penalty of spiritual death for all sinful humanity (Romans 3:23).

How Can One Man Die for Every Human?

One man Adam, by one brief sinful act, brought two kinds of death (separation from God) into existence for Adam and his descendants (Romans 5:17). First, Adam brought upon all humanity spiritual separation from God. Secondly, Adam brought upon himself and his descendants a physical separation of body and spirit, which is physical death. These "deaths" began when God cast the couple out of the Garden away from His presence and away from the Tree of Life (Genesis 3:24).

Jesus, by one physical death and by one brief spiritual separation from God, satisfied God's just punishment of sin and made possible God's forgiveness of sin (Matthew 27:46; Romans 3:21–26). The wages of sin is death and Jesus received this payment for all humanity! (Romans 6:23)

Jesus could do this because He Himself first existed in the form of God before the creation of the world (Philippians 2:6). By His Holy Spirit, God placed a young unborn child in the womb of a woman named Mary and the unique Son of God was born to her (Matthew 1:18–25; Galatians 4:4–5). God sent His Son to experience life as a human, so that He could die like a human both physically and spiritually (Hebrews 2:14–18). God then raised His Son from the dead, brought Him back, and proved that immortality of the soul is real (Matthew 16:21; 17:23). Furthermore, by Jesus's resurrection, God gave people assurance that Jesus is God's anointed Son (Romans 1:4; Acts 17:31). God also proved that His Son died on behalf of all of humanity from every generation through the ages, paying their penalty. Since Jesus, who had no sins, died for the sins of everyone, God can now forgive sinners and still be just. Forty days after Jesus's resurrection, He ascended to His Father and was seated at the Father's own right hand where He has been given authority to judge the world (Acts 17:31).

God's Love Will Not Forgive Some People

Jesus died and was raised for the forgiveness of human sin. However, the living, loving God of the Bible, the Creator of all mankind, will *not* forgive some people!

In the wilderness beside the Red Sea, Moses taught the Jewish people a song about God that included these words, "You in Your mercy have led forth the people whom You have redeemed" (Exodus 15:13, NKJV). Fourteen centuries before Jesus was born, God rescued Jesus's human ancestors from Egyptian slavery with ten mighty acts that are called the "ten plagues" (Exodus 7:14ff). Those mighty acts punished the Egyptians for their sins, but at the same time "saved" the Israelites from Egyptian slavery. Loving *mercy* prompted God's saving actions on behalf of the Jewish people. Loving *justice* prompted His punishable actions toward the Egyptians. *Mercy* and *justice* are two sides of God's one nature of love, and both were present in the ten plagues. But why did love make a difference between the Jewish people and the Egyptian people?

Not many days after composing the above-mentioned song, Moses climbed the mountain called Sinai. There the living Lord revealed many things about Himself. Exodus 34:5–7 lists some of the Lord's characteristics:

> Now the LORD descended in the cloud and stood with him [Moses] there, and proclaimed the name of the LORD. And the LORD passed before him and proclaimed, "The LORD, the LORD God, *loving and gracious*, longsuffering, and abounding in goodness and truth, keeping mercy for thousands, *forgiving iniquity and transgression and sin, by no means clearing the guilty* ..." (emphasis added)

God lovingly forgives iniquity, transgression, and sin, but He will not clear those He counts as guilty.

The two sides of love and the two sides of the God who is Love are seen in Exodus 34:5–7, written above. As discussed in previous chapters, the two sides of God's love are *mercy* on the one side and *justice* on the other. The Bible calls this the "goodness and severity of God" (Romans 11:22). On the one hand, God will lovingly forgive sin, but on the other hand God will not "clear" the guilty. The loving God can forgive, but He will also hold people accountable for their sins. Therefore, there must be some rationale by which God draws the line between those sinners whom He will forgive and those sinners whose guilt cannot be "cleared." The difference hangs upon a sinner's love of God and the sinner's humble willingness to obey the living God of love! It hangs upon what a sinner does with God's grace.

This difference in sinners was discussed by Jesus Christ (Luke 18:9). Jesus told about two men who went up to the temple to pray. One man was lovingly forgiven of his sins; the other man received no mercy. Jesus said the difference between the two men was their humility. He warned, "Every one that exalts himself shall be abased; and he that humbles himself shall be exalted" (Luke 18:14). Although these two men were members of the Jewish race, the loving God drew a distinction between them based on humble repentance.

If a man or woman has a humble, repentant heart, God will direct that sinner to the good news about His Son (John 7:17). Faith in God's loving plan of salvation comes by hearing the Word of God (Romans 10:17). God can forgive the sinner *when the sinner humbly believes and obeys God's plan for accepting sinners. The Bible calls this "obeying the gospel"* (2 Thessalonians 1:8; 1 Peter 4:17). Obeying God's rules of acceptance is also called "calling on the name of the Lord" (Romans 10:13; Acts 22:16). God's loving *plan* was to justly *forgive* the sins of every humble, believing, repentant, human being who is immersed "into Christ" (Galatians 3:26–27). Sinners must *believe* the good news about God's only begotten Son dying on the cross for their sins (Acts 8:36–37; 1 Corinthians 15:3) they must *repent* of their sins (Acts 2:37; Luke 13:3; Acts 17:30); they must *confess* their faith that the crucified Jesus is the Son of God who was raised from the dead (Acts 8:37); and they must *be immersed* in a watery grave in the name of Jesus Christ for the forgiveness of their sins (Acts 2:38; 8:38; 22:16; Colossians 2:12).

When the obedient person is raised from the watery

grave, the Lord adds him to Christ's church (Acts 2:47) and expects him to walk in "newness of life" (Romans 6:4). The obedient person is called "a new creation" (2 Corinthians 5:17). In a figure of speech, the sinner's sins are said to be "washed away" (Acts 22:16).

Yes; it is *real*; the living Creator loves His creation and has overcome sin and death. "God so loved the world that he gave his only begotten Son that whosoever believes in Him should not perish but should have everlasting life" (John 3:16). The loving God has announced the good news of the appearance of the savior Jesus Christ, who has abolished death and has brought to light immortality and an eternal life with God (2 Timothy 1:10).

Questions for Thought and Discussion

1. How is God's relationship with us similar to that of a parent and child? How is it different?
2. Does God's creation of humans show a need for us or a desire for us? Why?
3. How is our free will a proof of God's love for us?
4. How can God love all people and yet punish some people?
5. What are some things that will change in our lives when we develop an understanding of God's love for us?

I AM Truth

Chris Kemp

Truth is consistent; it never contradicts itself. In mathematics, parallel lines run side by side, never crossing or diverging. Parallel lines are as close at the end as they are at the beginning. So is truth. Truth parallels itself. It never crosses or contradicts; it never diverges or departs. The lines of truth are as close at the end as they are at the beginning.

When a teaching contradicts itself, it is not truth. When a teaching departs from God's word, it is not truth. Truth is indispensable to reality. Without truth, nothing is real. With truth, reality is certain and absolute. Truth is not subject to how one feels or thinks; therefore, truth is an objective standard. Truth is independent of what is culturally popular. Truth is not determined by majority vote. Truth is not predicated upon what one believes. Truth is independent of belief. The sky is above the land whether one believes it or not. Air encircles the planet regardless of how one feels about it. Truth needs not one's permission for existence. Truth exists whether acknowledged or not. Some will not acknowledge the process of photosynthesis in plants, but plants continue to take in carbon dioxide and release oxygen nonetheless. The truth of this process does not depend upon anyone's acceptance of it. Truth does not cease to exist because some illogical person rejects it. If footprints are found in the sand, the logical conclusion is that someone made those prints. One does not have to witness the making of those prints to know that someone or something made them.

So it is with God. All things have been made, and it is illogical to conclude that nothing made them. The creator of footprints does not cease to exist because someone illogically concludes He doesn't exist. "The heavens declare the glory of God; and the firmament shows his handiwork" (Psalm 19:1, NKJV). In other words, the universe is the fingerprint and footprint of God. The truth that God created all things does not cease to exist because someone illogically concludes otherwise. Such is other than wise. Such is foolishness. Again, truth does not need anyone's permission for existence. Neither a man's denial of truth nor rejection of it causes it to not exist. God is truth. The existence of the God of truth is not dependent upon someone's reception of Him. God doesn't fluctuate between existence and non-existence like a blinking neon light because someone may or may not believe in Him. God is real and so is truth. God is truth.

God is truth. All three members of the Godhead—consisting of the Father, Son, and the Holy Spirit (Matthew 28:18–20; 2 Corinthians 13:14)—are truth. All three members of the Godhead are truth. Moses said of Father

God: "He is the Rock, His work is perfect: for all his ways are justice, a God of truth and without injustice; righteous and upright is He" (Deuteronomy 32:4). Jesus Christ, the Son of God, is truth. He stated such in John 14:6: "I am the way, the truth, and the life. No one comes to the Father except through Me." The Holy Spirit of God is truth. "This is he who came by water and blood—Jesus Christ; not by water only, but by water and blood. And it is the Spirit who bears witness, because the Spirit is truth" (1 John 5:6). Since God is truth, He cannot lie (Numbers 23:10; Titus 1:2; Hebrews 6:18). The apostle John said: " ... no lie is of the truth" (1 John 2:21).

In the same way we accept that God is truth, we also can learn the opposite of this. In particular, we learn that Satan is the father of lies. Deceit is his native language. Jesus said the hypocrites of His day were the followers of Satan. Another word for Satan is the devil.

> You are of your father the devil, and the desires of your father you want to do. He was a murderer from the beginning, and does not stand in the truth, because there is no truth in him. When he speaks a lie, he speaks from his own resources, for he is a liar and the father of it (John 8:44).

The wicked devil has deceived most of the world with his lies. "We know that we are of God, and the whole world lies under the sway of the wicked one" (1 John 5:19).

Because of this, God says His people are to test what is taught. "Beloved, do not believe every spirit, but test the spirits, whether they are of God; because many false prophets have gone out in the world" (1 John 4:1). Again, God says His people are not to be gullible. "Test all things; hold fast what is good. Abstain from every form of evil" (1 Thessalonians 5:21–22). In the book of Acts, there was a group of people that tested what was taught to see if it was truth. They did not believe anyone without first checking the teaching with the truth of Scripture. Remember, truth parallels itself. It never contradicts. Listen to how they did it: "These were more fair-minded than those in Thessalonica, in that they received the word with all readiness, and *searched the Scriptures daily to find out whether these things were so*" (Acts 17:11).

Every person has the responsibility to test what is being taught. Does the teaching parallel what is right or does it contradict? Is it true or false? Is it right or wrong? "Be diligent to present yourself approved to God, a worker who does not need to be ashamed, rightly dividing the word of truth" (2 Timothy 2:15). One must be diligent as a student of Scripture to be able to know what is actually being taught. Satan and his worldly followers seek to manipulate a passage of Scripture to say it teaches something other than what is written. A single verse of Scripture never contradicts another. God does not contradict himself and neither does his word. In order to be able to "rightly divide" Scripture, one must know certain things.

First of all, one must know who is doing the speaking and to whom it is being spoken. If, for example, Genesis 3:4–5 were read, one would need to ask, "Who is doing the speaking and to whom is it being spoken?" The passage reads: "You shall not surely die. For God knows that in the day you eat of it your eyes will be opened, and you will be like God, knowing good and evil." In this passage, the devil appeared in the form of a serpent. He tempted Eve to eat what God had strictly forbidden. The serpent lied to Eve by telling her that she would not die if she ate. In order to "rightly divide" (2 Timothy 2:15) Scripture, one must understand that the devil is the one doing the speaking, and that Eve believed a lie and transgressed. If one fails to rightly divide Scripture and interpret it properly, one will think that all forbidden items may be eaten and enjoyed without consequence. Eve wasn't the only one who failed to understand the importance of rightly dividing the truth. The apostle Peter said there were some in the first century who were guilty of the same improper handling of Scripture:

> and consider that the longsuffering of our Lord is salvation - as also our beloved brother Paul, according to the wisdom given to him, has written to you, as also in all his epistles, speaking in them of these things, in which are some things hard to understand, which untaught and unstable people twist to their own destruction, as they do also the rest of the Scriptures (2 Peter 3:15–16).

God is absolute truth; therefore, His word is absolute truth. Psalm 19:7 says, "The law of the Lord is perfect, converting the soul." 1 Peter 1:24–25 speak of how the grass of the field fades in time, but "the word of the Lord endures forever." Many human laws change from generation to generation, but Psalm 119:89 says, "Forever, O Lord, your word is settled in heaven." The nature of God does not change (Hebrews 13:8) and neither does His infallible, perfect word (Hebrews 6:17). Humans change their feelings like the clouds above, but the word of God is the same forever. Both God and His word are absolute truth. Truth is truth, and it does not change.

Absolute truth is different from relative truth. Relative truth really is not truth at all because it changes from person to person. Relative truth suggests that something is true only to the one who believes it. For example, relative truth offers chastity as a virtue only for the one who seeks virtuous character. It is believed by proponents of relative truth that it is good to remain faithful to one's spouse only if one wants to remain faithful to one's spouse. But, for all those who believe it is good to cheat on one's spouse, then relative truth says dishonesty and lies are truth. One who espouses relative truth contends that his dishonest behavior in committing fornication against his spouse is not wrong. Believers in relative truth resent being told their sinful behavior is wrong. Relative truth advocates that wrong behavior is right because one wants it to be right. Wrong becomes right if one desires for wrong to be right. This is utterly foolish! Right is right, and wrong is wrong. God is absolute truth.

Morality and chastity are virtues because the eternal and all-wise God shows us that they are virtues. His perfect character exemplifies honesty and integrity as virtues. Fornication is always wrong, no matter how much a person desires for it to be right. Again, right is right, and wrong is wrong. We learn this by studying the nature of God and His holy word. God's word says in Hebrews 13:4 that "marriage is honorable in all and the bed undefiled, but whoremongers and adulterers God will judge." 1 Thessalonians 4:3 says, "For this is the will of God, your sanctification:

that you should abstain from sexual immorality." Nowhere in the Scriptures is it found that sexual immorality is sometimes acceptable! Fornication is always wrong. It is wrong if the rich commit it or if the poor commit it. It is wrong if the popular and powerful commit it or if the hermit and impoverished commit it. Wrong is wrong always, and right is right always.

Another example showing the fallacy of relative truth can be seen in the example of murder. As already mentioned, relative truth suggests that something wrong is actually right and true if someone wants it to be that way. If one were to espouse the theory of relative truth concerning murder, this would be the conclusion: "Murder is wrong if one believes it is wrong, but if one believes his own pleasure and happiness is the chief goal of life, then murdering someone who is not liked would be good." This is totally absurd, but this is how some view the world. Can you imagine a world where everyone thought this way? Can you fathom what our society would be like if it were acceptable to murder someone simply because that person was not liked? Many murderers rationalize their murder to the point that they feel justified in committing murder. They feel that their personal happiness is more important than the life of another human. One espousing relative truth would be forced to conclude that murder is right if one wanted it to be right! God's word says:

> Beloved, do not avenge yourselves, but rather give place to wrath, for it is written, "Vengeance is Mine, I will repay," says the Lord. Therefore "If your enemy is hungry, feed him; If he is thirsty, give him a drink; For in

so doing you will heap coals of fire on his head." Do not be overcome by evil, but overcome evil with good (Romans 12:19–21).

One may commit murder and not get caught by the authorities of the land, but God will judge every deed and this includes murder. Murder is wrong whether one gets caught or whether one feels good about it. Murder is wrong because the source of all truth, God, says it is wrong.

Truth is vitally important for a number of reasons. The most important aspect of truth is its ability to save humanity. Humans are sinners (Romans 3:23) and in need of salvation from our sins. No one is exempt from sin except Jesus Christ. For this reason, Jesus Christ is qualified to be our Savior. Hebrews 4:15 says of Christ, "For we do not have a High Priest who cannot sympathize with our weaknesses, but was in all points tempted as we are, yet without sin." When Jesus was upon the earth, He prayed to His Heavenly Father for His disciples saying, "Sanctify them by your truth. Your word is truth" (John 17:17). Humans are sanctified by God's truth, the word of God. Both sinners and saints are sanctified by God's word of truth. Sinners are sanctified or saved by truth. "Of His own will He brought us forth by the word of truth, that we might be a kind of firstfruits of His creatures" (James 1:18). Again, sinners are saved by truth. " ... you have purified your souls in obeying the truth through the Spirit ... having been born again, not of corruptible seed but incorruptible, through the word of God which lives and abides forever" (1 Peter 1:22–23). Jesus said: "And you shall know the truth, and the truth shall make you free" (John 8:32). Error does not save; it condemns. Sincerely believing a lie does not make something true. For example, you will recall the story of Joseph we discussed in chapter nine. Joseph's brothers sold him into slavery and told their father, Jacob, that Joseph's precious coat of many colors had been found. This coat, given to Joseph by their father, was covered in blood.

The brothers had actually killed a goat and poured the blood over the coat. The brothers deceived their father into thinking Joseph had been killed in the field by a wild beast. When Jacob saw the bloody coat he said: "It is my son's tunic. A wild beast has devoured him. Without doubt Joseph is torn to pieces" (Genesis 37:33). Joseph was not torn to pieces. He was alive and on his way to Egypt as a slave. Jacob had no doubt that his son was dead, but he was actually alive. In the same way, when someone sincerely believes something false, it is still false. Sincerity does not make a lie true. Jesus said in John 14:6: "I am the way, the truth, and the life. No one comes to the Father except through me." Someone may believe salvation can be through someone other than Jesus, but believing such does not change reality. The reality is that salvation is found only in Jesus Christ.

God is truth and His standard of judgment is according to truth. "But we know that the judgment of God is according to truth ... " (Romans 2:2). All men will appear before God one day to be judged according to their works. "And as it is appointed for men to die once, but after this the judgment" (Hebrews 9:27). This is the message of the apostle Paul: "For we must all appear before the judgment seat of Christ, that each one may receive the things done in the body, according to what he has done, whether good or bad" (2 Corinthians 5:10). The God of truth will judge the deeds of man with righteous and true judgment. Those who refuse to come to the truth of Jesus Christ for salvation will be judged and condemned.

> But in accordance with your hardness and your impenitent heart you are treasuring up for yourself wrath in the day of wrath and revelation of the righteous judgment of God, who will render to each according to his deeds (Romans 2:5–6).

Acts 17:30 says, "Truly, these times of ignorance God overlooked, but now commands all men everywhere to repent." One can clearly see that ignorance is no excuse for not doing what is true and right.

God is truth and the practice of the Christian is truth. When the apostle John spoke of those who will perish in Hell forever, he wrote of their character:

> But the cowardly, unbelieving, abominable, murderers, sexually immoral, sorcerers, idolaters, and all liars shall have their part in the lake which burns with fire and brimstone, which is the second death (Revelation 21:8).

Christians reject lies and deceit. When God described genuine love, He said:

> Love suffers long and is kind; love does not envy; love does not parade itself, is not puffed up; does not behave rudely, does not seek its own, is not provoked, thinks no

evil; does not rejoice in iniquity, but rejoices in the truth (1 Corinthians 13:4–6).

The apostle John said: "I have no greater joy than to hear that my children walk in truth" (3 John 4).

One is able to walk in truth when he sets his heart on what is true. If one chooses to take pleasure in lies, he will eventually believe a lie. It is very important to think on things that are true and right. Listen to what the apostle Paul said in Philippians 4:8

> Finally, brethren, whatever things are true, whatever things are noble, whatever things are just, whatever things are pure, whatever things are lovely, whatever things are of good report, if there is any virtue and if there is anything praiseworthy —meditate on these things.

When one follows this instruction and meditates on what is true and pure, he will put off the evil behaviors of the world. Ephesians 4:21 says that Christians will do this, "If indeed you have heard Him and have been taught by Him, as the truth is in Jesus." One is taught by Jesus's teachings when he spends time meditating on these teachings. Such is necessary for the Christian life.

God is truth and the worship of God is according to truth. For those who reject God, it is said of them that they "exchanged the truth of God for the lie, and worshiped and served the creature rather than the Creator" (Romans 1:25). In truth, God is the Creator and all of mankind is the created. Sticks and stone did not create the world.

> Therefore, since we are the offspring of God, we ought not to think that the Divine Nature is like gold or silver or stone, something shaped by art and man's devising. Truly, these times of ignorance God overlooked, but now commands all men everywhere to repent, because He has appointed a day on which He will judge the world in righteousness by the Man whom He has ordained. He has given assurance of this to all by raising Him from the dead (Acts 17:29–31).

Men who worship the creature rather than the Creator profess to be wise, but really are fools. "Professing to be wise, they became fools" (Romans 1:22).

Once man realizes that God is the Creator, he is to worship Him in spirit and in truth. Jesus said: "God is Spirit, and those who worship Him must worship in spirit and truth" (John 4:24). The human spirit must be sincerely humble before God when he worships. Also, humans must worship according to the truth of God's word. God tells us how to worship. Humans do not tell God how to be worshipped.

> And let the peace of God rule in your hearts, to which also you were called in one body; and be thankful. Let the word of Christ dwell in you richly in all wisdom, teaching and admonishing one another in psalms and hymns and spiritual songs, singing with grace in your hearts to the Lord. And whatever you do in word or

deed, do all in the name of the Lord Jesus, giving thanks to God the Father through Him (Colossians 3:15–17).

Worship is to be offered according to the New Testament authority of Jesus Christ's truth. We know how to worship God based on the truth of the Bible. In particular, the New Testament teaches Christians how God chooses to be worshipped. The New Testament informs Christians how they are to serve God. It is the truth of Jesus Christ's covenant that instructs Christians on what God expects from their lives. However, the devil seeks to distort God's teaching and deceive people into following lies instead. God foretold of when people would tum away from sound, healthy doctrine.

> For the time will come when they will not endure sound doctrine, but according to their own desires, because they have itching ears, they will heap up for themselves teachers; and they will tum their ears away from the truth, and be turned aside to fables (2 Timothy 4:3–4).

Christians must be diligent in their study of the truth. Many lies and fables will deceive. Beware of any teaching that suggests that God will accept any kind of worship whatsoever if it is offered sincerely. Sincerely believing a lie does not make something true and right.

In conclusion, when we become interested in learning about the true God and what He desires from humanity, we begin to realize that we can turn to the Bible as God's book. It is the authority that God has provided for us as humans to look to so that we can begin to understand God and His truth. God is truth, and there is nothing contradictory either about Him or His word. The closer an individual walks with the God of truth, the more spiritually enriched his life will be. The further away an individual strays from God, the less spiritually enriched his life will be. If one worships and follows the world, he will become worldly. If one chooses rather to worship and follow God, he will become godly. Godly people are people of truth because they follow the God of truth. Jesus Christ invites all people everywhere to follow him as He leads us to true living and true reward. Will you follow the God of truth?

Questions for Thought and Discussion

1. Is it possible for God to be untruthful? Why or why not?
2. How can we determine truth through the Scriptures?
3. How has the concept of relative truth affected our society today?
4. In what way is it truth that makes us free, as stated in John 8:32?
5. How does the knowledge of God's unchanging truth affect the way we approach worship?

I AM Eternal

Ted Burleson

Introduction

The concept of eternity is very difficult to understand because we, as hmnan beings, are subject to time. Everything and everyone except God, His Son, and His Holy Spirit had a beginning. It may help us to remember that eternity, like God, did not have a beginning and it will never end. No boundaries can be placed on God by assigning Him a specific place and time. Likewise, His duration is endless. His eternal nature excels all times and durations. God always remains the same and does not change. James explained that with God, there is "no variation or shadow due to change" (James 1:17).

In addition to eternity in the sense of timeless duration, eternity is also beyond anything that we know in this world. Nothing that we know of in this world belongs to the next world other than God and the spirit of human beings, because once created (born), humans live forever.

God exists now and since He has no past and will never cease to exist, He is eternal. In other words, God is timeless. It was undoubtedly this attribute of God that the four creatures in the Book of Revelation that were gathered around the throne of God had in mind when they said, "Holy, holy, holy, the Lord God the Almighty, who was and is, and is to come" (Revelation 4:8).

God, Unlike Human Beings, is Eternal

Paul recognized this fact when he wrote to Timothy, "It is he alone who has immortality and dwells in unapproachable light, whom no one has ever seen or can see; to him be honor and eternal dominion" (1 Timothy 6:16). The human view of eternity is like seeing only a photograph of a single series of events from our viewpoint in time. However, when God looks at eternity, it is as if He views it from the top of a tower or high mountain. Rather than seeing only a snapshot in time, God sees all eternity in one instant. For the sake of comparison, it is as if we were like an ant trying to comprehend how large the earth is, while on the other hand God is looking down on the earth from space clearly seeing the size of the earth. God's ways are not like our ways.

Regarding time, God can say, "I was," "I am," "I shall be," or even "I will do." With respect to His own existence, He says, "I am." As Moses tried to make excuses as to why he should not return to Egypt to lead his people out of bondage, he complained that the people would ask, "Who sent you?" God replied, "I AM WHO I AM. He said further, 'I AM has sent me to you'" (Exodus 3:14). Calling

God the Great "I AM" involves eternity, for God has always existed and will always exist, therefore, He is. The description of God using the present tense, "I Am," shows that His essence knows no past, nor is it limited by the future. For God to say that His name is "I Am" indicates that He always was and always will be present.

God Has Always Existed

God did not begin, therefore He will never grow old and He will never die or have an end. God caused creation to come into existence, but God Himself is uncaused. No one or no thing created God, for His existence is unending. He has always existed and will always exist. There has never been a time when God did not exist, and there will never be a time when God does not exist.

The people of the Old Testament recognized God's eternal nature. Abraham, who is often called the father of our faith, once solemnized a covenant with Abimelech by planting a tree in Beersheba and calling on the El Olam ("Everlasting God"). Genesis 21:33 describes this event. "Abraham planted a tamarisk tree in Beersheba, and called there on the name of the LORD, the Everlasting God." David, one of the writers of the Old Testament Book of Psalms, recognized God's eternal nature and writes, "The LORD sits enthroned as king forever" (Psalm 29:10). David also wrote about God, "Your years have no end" (Psalm 102:27). Another Psalm records the words, "This is God, our God forever and ever. He will be our guide forever" (Psalm 48:14). Moses quotes God Himself saying that He will live forever (Deuteronomy 32:40). Perhaps

Moses had this thought in mind when he later wrote, "Before the mountains were brought forth, or ever you had formed the earth and the world, from everlasting to everlasting you are God" (Psalm 90:2). Daniel refers to God as "the Ancient One," or in Aramaic, the "Ancient of Days" (Daniel 7:9). Because God had no beginning and created all things through Jesus Christ, He was present before days and time began.

Like their Old Testament counterparts, several of the individuals found in the New Testament also recognize God's eternal nature. Included in Paul's first letter to Timothy, as Paul encourages Timothy to use Paul's ministry as an example, he gives glory to God. Paul writes, "To the King of the ages, immortal, invisible, the only God, be honor and glory forever and ever" (1 Timothy 1:17). Jude, whom we believe to be Jesus's half-brother, writes by God's guidance in his little book, "To the only God our Savior, through Jesus Christ our Lord, be glory, majesty, power, and authority, before all time and now and forever" (Jude 25).

Before any other reality existed, God was present in His timeless eternity; therefore, the universe has not always existed. Genesis 1:1–2, the first sentence of the Old Testament, says, "In the beginning when God created the heavens and the earth, the earth was a formless void and darkness covered the face of the deep, while a wind from God swept over the face of the waters." As long as humans have lived there has been evidence for God's eternal nature because of the observable creation. Paul wrote to the Roman Christians, "Ever since the creation of the world his eternal power and divine nature, invisible though they are, have been understood and seen through the things he has made" (Romans 1:20).

All of the attributes of God that are discussed in this book depend upon the eternal nature of God. If God is not eternal, then none of the claims of Christianity have any significance. Even those that would reject the eternal nature of God because of unbelief are without excuse, for evidence of His existence is all around us in the created world. God has made it plain, even to unbelievers, because He has shown His eternal nature through creation. Romans 1:18–19 says,

> For the wrath of God is revealed from heaven against all ungodliness and wickedness of those who by their wickedness suppress the truth. For what can be known about God is plain to them, because God has shown it to them.

God is Not Limited By Time Nor Under the Law of Time

Time means nothing to God. Time is just the way that human beings measure days and seasons; it cannot be used to measure God's existence. Peter urged his readers, "But do not ignore this one fact, beloved, that with the Lord one day is like a thousand years, and a thousand years are like one day" (2 Peter 3:8). God is the source and ground of all reality. He set time in motion when He created the earth, the sun, the moon, and the stars. He set the seasons into a cycle of rotation. This observable, changing world is very important, for the eternal God created it and human beings live in it.

Creation is not eternal; it had a beginning. Human beings and even angels are created beings, so neither humans nor angels are eternal in the sense of having always existed. Since God did not have a beginning, time cannot apply to Him. Humans mark time to note the duration of an event or a succession of events. However, God cannot be marked by time for He had no beginning and no end. God's age cannot be measured, for time does not pertain to Hirn. This explains God's statement through Isaiah, "I am God, and there is no one like me, declaring the end from the beginning, and from ancient time things not yet done" (Isaiah 46:9b–10).

After discussing a time for everything under the sun, the writer of Ecclesiastes explains that although humans cry for life without change, our own mortality reminds us that change is inevitable among humans. "He has made everything suitable for its time; moreover he has put a sense of past and future into their minds, yet they cannot find out what God has done from the beginning to the end" (Ecclesiastes 3:11). Only God knows what has happened in eternity for only God has been present before time began.

The Eternal Nature of God Allows Him to Give Out Eternal Life

Everything that had a beginning is physical and not eternal. Because it is physical and not eternal, every created thing will die physically. John made this very plain in 1 John 2:17,

"And the world and its desire are passing away, but those who do the will of God live forever." Although we will all die physically, we can live spiritually with God for eternity. Much of the Bible has to do with God's eternal principles and plans that relate to humans.

There are great differences between humans and God because we are so vastly unlike Him. However, even though there are vast differences between the Creator and the creation, because of His unsurpassed love, He bridges the gap between Himself and humans with the bridge of grace, constructed on the sacrifice of the life and blood of Jesus Christ. We can then cross God's "bridge" called grace by "crossing over" through our obedient faith.

Why does God love humanity? Humans are so different from God—why would He love us? Any kinship between humans and God is of God's making and not from human efforts. In our sinful state, we do not deserve to even be associated with God. Because we are so unworthy to commune with God, we must have God's divine grace. Without God's grace, we cannot be justified and be forgiven of our sins. God, unlike humans, is the supreme embodiment of goodness, mercy, and kindness. He opposed evil because He is the ultimate good.

Those who live in sin are spiritually dead, but those who live in Christ are alive spiritually. Paul wrote, "For the wages of sin is death, but the free gift of God is eternal life in Christ Jesus our Lord" (Romans 6:23). It is only through Jesus Christ that humans have the hope of eternal life. Jesus "abolished death and brought life and immortality to light through the gospel" (2 Timothy 1:10). It is only through responding to the Gospel of Jesus Christ that humans have any hope of living eternally without separation from God. Every person not in Christ will experience eternal disaster.

Every human being will be living forever, either with God in heaven or away from God in hell. Time will be no more but eternity will always exist. All humans had a beginning. God created Adam and Eve, the first man and woman, and all humanity descended from them. Individually, we all had a birthday, a beginning. God has no birthday, no beginning, for He has always existed. If God had a beginning, then He would be dependent upon a divine parent or another power greater than Himself. He is dependent upon no one. One of Job's friends, Elihu, explains the eternal nature of God by saying that "the number of his years is unsearchable" (Job 36:26).

We are unlike God in that we had a beginning and He did not have a beginning. However, we are like God in the sense that we will have no end. Knowing this fact, Moses pleaded with God, "Who considers the power of your anger? Your wrath is as great as the fear that is due you. So teach us to count our days that we may gain a wise heart" (Psalm 90:11–12).

The Eternal God Has Spoken to Humans By His Son, Jesus Christ

"Long ago God spoke to our ancestors in many and various ways by the prophets, but in these last days he has spoken to us by a Son, whom he appointed heir of all things, through whom he also created the worlds" (Hebrews 1:1–3). This "Son" is Jesus, being God in human flesh. Jesus, as

God in human form, walked the earth at one point and place in time to demonstrate for humans of all times how to live as God would have us to live. If Jesus is God in the flesh, who revealed himself to humanity in space and time, then how do we find out about this? There is only one source to tell us about these events. These events are recorded in God's divine revelation, the Bible. From this account of Jesus, we learn that there are not many ways to God; there's only one way to live eternally with God. Jesus said, "I am the way, and the truth, and the life. No one comes to the Father except through me" (John 14:6). This truth about Jesus is found only in the Bible. "There is salvation in no one else, for there is no other name under heaven given among mortals by which we must be saved" (Acts 4:12).

Although we cannot undo the sins of the past, by God's grace in Christ Jesus we are justified and acquitted of our past sins. We can't work enough to earn salvation. Not enough mantras could ever be stated to earn us a place in heaven. Regardless of the stances and prostrations, we may take in our worship, we cannot be saved without God's grace. Grace is God's free gift to those who follow and obey Jesus while seeking to have a relationship with God through Jesus. Grace doesn't mean the expansion of the human self and submersion in the divine. Grace includes God's entire plan for saving humanity eternally, including the fact that God sent His Son, Jesus, to die for humans. He was raised from the dead and ascended back into heaven. God's words, found in the Bible, direct us to obedience and a lifestyle modeled after God. We are not mere spectators in the drama called grace. We are active participants living our lives in ways that please God. Our eternal destinations are determined by our response to God's grace.

Conclusion

The eternity of God should be a source of great comfort to Christians. If God had a beginning, then He would also have an end and our hopes for living eternally with Him would end along with our Christian joy. Humans are in a continual state of flux. Change is an everyday occurrence in the lives of human beings. Whether change comes about by a natural progression over the years or suddenly because of an accident, human beings change. A grown man is the same person as the little boy, but his characteristics have changed considerably. On the other hand, God does not change. The Lord is the same and His "years will never end" (Hebrews 1:12).

Because God is eternal, His covenant with Christians is likewise eternal. Although physical death occurs to all humanity, "the trumpet will sound, and the dead will be raised imperishable, and we will be changed" (1 Corinthians 15:52). "Then we who are alive, who are left, will be caught up in the clouds together with them [the dead in Christ] to meet the Lord in the air; and so we will be with the Lord forever" (1 Thessalonians 4:17). Jesus said,

> Do not be astonished at this; for the hour is coming when all who are in their graves will hear his voice and will come out—those who have done good, to the resur-

rection of life, and those who have done evil, to the resurrection of condemnation (John 5:28–29).

Because God is eternal, threats against the church by her enemies will exist only for a limited time. Jesus promised concerning His church, "The gates of Hades will not prevail against it" (Matthew 16:18). Although we cannot fully comprehend God's eternal nature, we can understand that God has an eternal nature. He is the first cause of all that exists. The difference in the brevity of human life and the eternal nature of God is often illustrated by a tree standing beside water (consider Psalm 1:1–3). The tree stands in the same place, unmoved by the waters of the river. In contrast, the water in the river continually moves in a fluid motion by the tree, without changing the position of the tree. Likewise, God stands unmoved by time while humans are in continual flux brought about by change.

Our eternal God is worthy of worship and our endless service. No human is worthy of our worship, but the eternal God who created the earth and all that is good in it is worthy of our worship and adoration. Christians should have the attitude of the psalmist, "I will sing to the LORD as long as I live; I will sing praise to my God while I have my being" (Psalm 104:33). Thank God that He is eternal. Obey His will so that you may live eternally with Him in heaven.

Questions for Thought and Discussion

1. Why is the concept of eternity so difficult for humans to grasp?
2. As it relates to His eternal nature, what is the significance of God calling Himself "I AM"?
3. Why is it essential for believers to recognize the eternal nature of God?
4. How does God's concept of time affect the church?
5. Are humans eternal creatures? Why or why not?

Scripture Index

Contributors

Bill Bagents (DMin Amridge University), is Professor of Ministry, Counseling and Biblical Studies at Heritage Christian University, Florence, Alabama.

Jeremy W. Barrier (PhD Brite Divinity School, Texas Christian University) is Professor of Biblical Literature at Heritage Christian University, Florence, Alabama. He is also the director of a global evangelism program entitled "World Mission" for the Madison church of Christ, Madison, Alabama.

Joseph A. Barrier (MMin Heritage Christian University) is a fulltime missionary for the World Evangelism program under the oversight of the Double Springs church of Christ, Double Springs, Alabama.

Wayne Barrier (MS University of Tennessee) He serves on the Heritage Christian University Board of Directors and directs a mission program under the oversight of the Double Springs church of Christ, Double Springs, Alabama.

Ted Burleson (DMin Harding School of Theology), is the pulpit minister for the Hamilton church of Christ, Hamilton, Alabama and a professor at Amridge University, Montgomery, Alabama.

Cory Collins (MAR Westminster Theological Seminary) is the pulpit minister for the Keller Church of Christ, Keller, Texas.

Edmon L. Gallagher (PhD Hebrew Union College), is Professor of Christian Scripture at Heritage Christian University, Florence, Alabama.

Chris Kemp is the pulpit minister for the Northside Church of Christ in Mayfield, Kentucky.

Brad McKinnon (PhD in progress Aberdeen University) is Associate Professor of History, Managing Editor of HCU Press, and Director of Christian Service at Heritage Christian University, Florence, Alabama.

Larry Murdock (MAR Harding School of Theology) serves as minister for the Gandy church of Christ in Lawrenceburg, Tennessee and he writes, records, and produces gospel messages for Voice of Truth World Wide Radio Evangelism.

David H. Warren (ThD Harvard University), is an independent scholar. He is coeditor of *Early Christian Voices: In Texts, Traditions, and Symbols* (2003).

Charles R. Webb (EdD Auburn University) is a retired Associate Professor of Psychology from Freed-Hardeman University, Henderson, Tennessee.

Kevin J. Youngblood (PhD Southern Baptist Theological Seminary) is a professor at Harding University, Searcy, Arkansas.

Credits

Also by Cypress Publications

Always Near: Listening for Lessons from God

by Bill Bagents

The Christian Life: Chapters for Bible Teacher

by Ed Gallagher

Cruciform Christ: 52 Reflections on the Gospel of Mark

by Travis Bookout

Easing Life's Hurts 2nd ed.

by Jack Wilhelm and Bill Bagents

Equipping the Saints: A Practical Study of Ephesians 4:11–16

by Bill Bagents and Cory Collins

The Holy Spirit: A Bible Study Guide

by Jack Wilhelm

Jesus the Christ: Chapters for Bible Teachers

by Ed Gallagher

King of Glory: 52 Reflections on the Gospel of John

by Travis Bookout

Rescue: God and Sin in the Old Testament

by John F. Wakefield

Revisiting Life's Oases: Soul-Soothing Stories

by Bill Bagents

Welcoming God's Word: Reading with Head and Heart

by Bill Bagents

WHAM! Facing Life's Heavy Hits: Thirteen Old Testament Encounters

by Bill and Laura S. Bagents

WHAM! Facing Life's Heavy Hits: Thirteen New Testament Encounters

by Bill and Laura S. Bagents

Women in the Shadows

by Betty Hamblen

CYPRESS

To see full catalog of Heritage Christian University Press
and its imprint Cypress Publications, visit
www.hcu.edu/publications

www.ingramcontent.com/pod-product-compliance
Lightning Source LLC
Chambersburg PA
CBHW071322120626
46546CB00002B/404